THE PERFECT LAW

THE DEFINITIVE ANSWER TO
THAT AGE OLD QUESTION
"WHY DID THIS HAPPEN?"

LIBERTY
THE
PERFECT LAW

THE DEFINITIVE ANSWER TO
THAT AGE OLD QUESTION
"WHY DID THIS HAPPEN?"

by Michael Angelo

A ZUGOS PUBLICATION

Copyright © 2006 by Michael Angelo ISBN #978-0-9788354-0-8
Library of Congress Catalog Number pending.

ISBN-10: 0-9788354-0-9
ISBN-13: 978-0-9788354-0-9

All rights reserved national and international. No portion of this book may be reproduced, stored in any retrieval system, or transmitted in any form or by any means—electronic, mechanical, audio, or visual—without the prior written and expressed permission of the publisher. The exceptions are the brief quotations used in critical reviews, or articles of review.

Published by Zugos Publishing, LLC. P.O. Box 1738, Westerville, Ohio 43086-1738

Contents

Dedications		vii
Preface		ix
CHAPTER 1	The Calling	1
CHAPTER 2	Laws and Rules *Law • The Genesis of the Law • I AM / i am •* *Absolute Law • Universal Law • Rules*	7
CHAPTER 3	Spiritual Law	19
CHAPTER 4	Understanding the Bible as History *Perfect Interpretation • Imperfect Interpretation •* *Controversy • All Knowing God • Eliminating* *Contradictions • Gone With The Wind*	25
CHAPTER 5	The Teacher	39
CHAPTER 6	Getting Started *Sin • Iniquity • Transgression • Trespass • Deed*	45
CHAPTER 7	Making it Real *II Samuel 11 • II Samuel 12*	53
CHAPTER 8	Judgement *King David's Plight*	61
CHAPTER 9	S/spirit and Perfection *S/spirit • Perfection • Blamelessness*	75
CHAPTER 10	The Constitution of The Perfect Law of Liberty *Bilateral Law • The Governor (Standard* *of Measure)*	83

CHAPTER 11	Mastering the Perfect Law of Liberty	93
CHAPTER 12	Some Necessary Side-Bars and Notes	99
CHAPTER 13	The Advocate	117
CHAPTER 14	The Anomalies of The Perfect Law of Liberty *Unwarranted Law • Generational Law •* *Friends and Influences • Unfruitful* *Covenants • The Summation of Deed Creation*	121
CHAPTER 15	Deed Recompense	135
Conclusion		145
Appendix		147
Acknowledgments		149
About the Author		151

Dedications

To my Mother, who taught me what she could from her own treasure trove of wisdom, and then taught me *I could* learn the rest on my own.

To Dr. Inez W. Curry, who with a steady hand from her highschool "pulpit," without ever opening a Bible, taught me *I should* know God.

To the Reverend James (Jimmy) Marcum who introduced me to the Lord of Creation.

To Bishop Malcolm Smith, who gave content to my Biblical and spiritual education. For more than thirty years, Bishop Smith has been an invaluable inspiration to me. I consider Bishop Smith to be the greatest English-speaking teacher of our time. As a theologian, he is a leading authority on the subject of *covenant,* and in particular, the *Blood Covenant.* I believe his catalog of cassette, video, and CD albums present one of the most comprehensive educations that can be offered to a disciple of Christ. www.Malcolmsmith.org

My sincerest thank you to all of my most dedicated editors who gave of themselves beyond measure to encourage me onward and to advance this message; among them, Lead Technical Editors Georgia Lang and Kim Anthony; Content Editors Maria and Kris Domich, Melody and Nathan Keenan, Tim Wegner, Robert (Bob) Leone, the late Clifford Birt (2006), and Bill (Apple) Mihaltian; Printing assistance, Christopher Foy, Lynn Christel, and Matt Sosnowski of Banta Book Group; Manuscript preparation, Data Management Inc., Jeff Nelson Pres., Dave Sanders, Connie Wolfe, and Mike Moellers; Cover and logo art and design Troy Gillogly; the many others who over the years have read and/or encouraged this work but humbly declined mention.

Finally to the love of my life and my most devoted acolyte, my wife Sharon, whose tireless efforts have allowed me time to finish this work.

Preface

Why? *Why* is but a single word question, yet *why* is the most powerful question one can ask. It is a question as old as time itself. It has been asked repeatedly by every free-thinking, free-willed individual born to every generation from the beginning until now. If every minute of the creation story had been documented in the Holy Bible, I believe we would see that *Why* was a primary question asked often by the first man, Adam, in the Garden of Eden.

The all-encompassing answer to the question *why* is ***cause***. Over the passage of time man has added the prefix ***be*** as if to suggest there must *be* a *cause* to every *why*. Children seem trapped in a world of wonder and beg the question *why* circuitously as parents hem-haw toward the generic *because* as a means to quell their curiosities. On the other end of the spectrum, the more learned scientist, mathematician, or theorist will be most diligent to search out *the cause* for the reason *why* a phenomenon occurred. He or she knows that in science, there is always a fundamental law behind every process.

If there is a fundamental law behind every scientific process, why should anyone assume there is not also a fundamental law to explain all *cause* so that man may understand the *why* of every event? Why should we not know the reason children die, or the reason why some people find unwarranted success and prosperity while others seem bound to failure despite hard work, or why catastrophic events occur, such as natural events like tsunamis, earthquakes, and hurricanes as well as staged events like 9/11?

If there is a fundamental law behind all cause, then to date, mankind seems to have missed it inasmuch as many of the unexplainable events of life remain unexplained. "Experts" are continuously attempting to decipher why events unfold the way they do, but most offerings seem only to be educated opinions slanted toward the speaker's agenda, destitute, or at least lacking in insight and/or accuracy. Such opinions have yet to acknowledge any one fundamental law behind all events.

Notwithstanding, a law to explicate every event does exist, and the knowledge of this law has always been readily available to any treasure hunter in search of that elusive prize. It is a unifying law that brings the resources of Heaven and Earth together to answer the *"Why did this happen?"* question for each specific event of our lives. This law is seen in application throughout the entire Holy Bible. The name attributed to it therein can be found in the Book of James, chapter 1, verse 25. It is called **The Perfect Law of Liberty.** Allusions to the Perfect Law, and the attributes of this Law revealed in the Holy Bible, begin at the Garden of Eden and appear all through the Bible, making the existence of the Perfect Law irrefutable. Once this Law is identified and understood from the Bible, its existence becomes conspicuous throughout all world history, because this Law, The Perfect Law of Liberty, is the fundamental Law behind all cause.

Uncovering any buried treasure is a lengthy, meticulous process of prodding, digging, and sweeping away the layers of dust to reveal each portion of the treasure, and then identifying, mapping, and logging the hunt. Such work is best left to those called to the task, and future treasure hunters can appreciate the reports of those who went before and spared them some of the shovel and dust-brush work. Within the pages of this simple, easy-to-read volume, lies the report of one such discovery. This text lays the groundwork for the revelation of The Perfect Law of Liberty—the definitive answer to that age old question: *Why?*

Herein, this Law is revealed and its attributes and purposes set forth to be examined, evaluated, and assessed by those who are looking for answers. To support the proclamations made in this report, I include current events, and I refer to **historical data** recorded in the **King James Version** of the Holy Bible. This is my Bible of choice and the one I use in reference throughout this work. For simplicity, I often use the words "man," "he," and "him" to refer to "humankind," both male and female.

In this study we will bring to review some religious ideologies that may be suspect. I suggest that more than a few theological inaccuracies have entered mainstream thinking as attempts to explain why events unfold the way they do. These may have been well intended when they were introduced but are in need of much reexamination. For instance, it is often suggested that God is behind the negative events on the earth, that it is He who brings His disasters to punish us, or that He encumbers some of us with sickness, poverty, or suffering in order to teach us some lesson we lack. I suggest this "Act-of-God" ideology is insensitively offered and serves only to incite fear of God, driving those who are seeking answers further from the only One who can deliver absolute truth to them. Unfortunately, it has been a preoccupation of some religionists to use fear to enlist the inexperienced and naive into a religion.

Religion is not a church and religion is not a truth. Religion is a methodology employed to bring people to a church or to a truth. Religion is a man-invention established to emulate the first "church," the priesthood and temple worship of the Old Testament Hebrew people as it was designed by Jehova-Elohim, the LORD-God of the Hebrews. The format of buildings and leaders has become so diverse in modern eras as to gather people together into "church buildings" on worship days to discuss religious ideologies, some of which have nothing at all to do with a relationship with God. Consequently, any explanation offered by religion to explain the cause behind all events should be suspect. Likewise, any explanation offered by finite man (I include myself) to explain such a mystery of God-the-Infinite must also be suspect. We should be constantly questioning what we believe and how we have come to believe it. If there is a true answer to such a universal question as to why events unfold the way they do, that answer will be universally true; it will transcend all stations, and it will be evidentially apparent and observable in action and/or deed.

The prophets of old received their messages from God and then delivered those messages to the people (Numbers 12:5-8a). God had a rule to govern His message going forth, ensuring it was His truth that would be heard. If what a prophet spoke forth did not come to pass, then it should be assumed that prophet was not empowered by Jehovah-Elohim, and what he prophesied did not come from an omniscient and omnipotent God. False prophets could not be trusted, nor could their prophecies be trusted as true. As a consequence, the prophets who delivered false prophecies were to be eliminated (Deut. 18:17-22).

The New Testament is not so harsh toward teachers like myself who attempt to share spiritual truth. However, in the Book of James, we are warned not to be in a hurry to be a teacher (James 3:1). James told us the teacher would receive the greater condemnation. Jesus, speaking to those who lead, said it would be better to take a large millstone, hang it around the neck and toss oneself into the depths of the sea than to face judgement, guilty of having led another away from the truth of God (Matthew 18:6, Mark 9:2, and Luke 16:31).

We do not need a religion, this book, or a church to find truth. God was loving us before time began, and has been calling us to Himself every minute of every hour since the moment of our birth. Finding Him, knowing Him, and discerning His truth are the simplest and easiest things we can do. The way has been provided in abundance, and the knowledge to that way is innate in every living thing (Romans 1:20.).

Our innate spiritual knowledge includes the constitution of **The Perfect Law of Liberty** (herein referred to also as **the Perfect Law** for brevity). The Perfect Law is God's designed tool for bringing about love, joy, peace, success and prosperity, and for making life fair and equal for everybody. Because it is subtly known and little appreciated in our day, it is my purpose to present the Perfect Law, or better yet, to re-present it with words that will allow each of us to assemble the scattered pieces of knowledge we already hold into one logical, sound understanding that we may use to enable this tool to work for us.

The Bible teaches plainly that *ye need not that any man teach you* ... 1 John 2:27. Although this verse in the New Testament, declared after the resurrection of Jesus, is dedicated to those who have received the Anointing by believing in the Lord Jesus Christ, other scriptures show us God was present in the lives of men long before any event involving the man Jesus took place (Jer. 1:5, Isa. 49:5, Job 12:10). One of the purposes of the verse in 1 John, chapter 2, is to shed light on the fact that it is **God Himself**, through His Spirit, Who **teaches man**. We need not **depend** on any other. This is the way of God, and God has always operated in this fashion (Prov. 16:9). No one is outside of the unconditional love of God. We each have access to God's love and thereby, His wisdom (James1:5) and knowledge (Proverbs 2:1-3).

It must also be said that although we need no man to teach us, the Bible declares we should not forsake the assembling together of ourselves (Hebrews 10:25). When we come together to share, knowledge increases. Without our sharing of the knowledge God has given us individually, we may not be able to achieve our fullness corporately, nor may we receive our own individual lessons that God speaks to each of us through the corporate body. God employs us all. Part of our purpose as we travel the road of life in this earthly reality is to help others along the way. Each of us is a necessary instrument of God, every one of us to some other person. We need to come together often in order to experience God's presence in our lives in this way, and to grow in our knowledge of God and of His designs for mankind.

Assembling ourselves together to learn about God is important to our knowing God and to finding our specific purpose for being (Matt. 18:20). We each have a specific purpose in this life, even those who believe themselves unworthy(Exodus 9:16 K.J.V. was spoken to Pharaoh). We can fulfill our purpose perfectly only by knowing God's will for us. Knowledge of God, and fellowship with one another as well as with God, will help to guide us to that place where we should be.

It is important that we know what we are supposed to do in this life, and that we do it according to God's design and will, because everything we do—every deed we create along the way—has consequences.

Preface

It is a little discussed matter in our places of worship that one day, each and every person, from every walk of life, and every belief and unbelief will have to stand before the throne of Grace and give account for the deeds he or she performed while on the Earth. Each and every one of us will be judged for our works because the deeds we perform while in the flesh have ramifications. The choices we make each day create the deeds we leave behind. Like living entities, the deeds we create continue to **improve** or **impair** the world we touched, and they do so long after we exit the arena in which they are created.

The Bible establishes that no man can be made clean enough or pure enough to become one with God based solely on his own ability to obey God's law. In other words, men are not justified before God by the deeds or the works they perform. Men are justified by their faith (Romans 3:21-28). Although men are justified by faith (Romans 1:17, Galatians 2:16), we need action or works (deeds) to validate that faith, to show it exists. Without works, faith is a corpse—it is dead. It is the work produced as a result of our faith in God that proves our faith real (James 2:14-26). God created the Law of Faith to govern our justification and reconciliation. He made the Perfect Law of Liberty to govern our deeds.

Knowing all things—knowing the heart of man, knowing He created man for good but man's propensity toward selfishness could lead him astray—God set into motion the Perfect Law to govern all of man's deeds, both the positive and the negative, the unselfish and the selfish. This Law is perfect in that it justly rewards or punishes **every** deed we accomplish, and does so without passion and without prejudice. The Law rewards every God-centered or positive deed, and the same Law punishes all self-centered or negative deeds.

The Perfect Law is commonly known among us. We all know it exists and we all know it works because our knowledge of the Perfect Law is innate to our spirit. This Law is so familiar among all people of the world, and is so prevalent to every language and social order, that we gloss over it in our everyday activities and reduce it to common cliches as if the Perfect Law is a myth.

So common among us is this Law that each of us has spoken the fundamental premise of the Perfect Law at some point in our lifetime. Simply stated, this Law declares, *"What goes around, comes around,"* or better yet, *"you will reap what you sow."* These phrases trip off our lips so easily, but have we ever seriously assessed their content or have they become merely offhand observations? If we desire to use the Perfect Law of Liberty to our advantage, we need to examine this Law as we never have before. The pages that follow will help to decipher this Law. We will see it is God who created the Perfect Law. We will see when the Law was introduced, why it was instituted, and how it was designed to work. We will discover examples of how the Law works when it is used properly, and examine what happens when the Law is ignored.

There is a Godly design for this Law beyond what we most often see. Primarily, the Perfect Law is a God-designed tool created to encourage Godliness in mankind. The Perfect Law causes love, joy, peace, and prosperity to develop and flourish in the lives of men and women who recognize the Law's power and potential, and understand how to use it properly. The secondary purpose for the Perfect Law is to make life fair, equal, and balanced for every person on Earth. The Law does so by administering discipline, limiting or eliminating any adversary that attempts to prevent justice.

A double-edged sword is a tool we can use hew the wood for the fire that warms us. However, if we ignore the sword's potential and use it carelessly, that same sword can cut us in half on the back swing. Likewise, the Perfect Law is a double-edged tool. In the hands of the man or woman who knows how to wield it, it will deliver promise. If neglected or abused, the Perfect Law will deliver punishment to correct our carelessness.

Justice and equity have run amuck throughout the world in our day. Mankind is experiencing the disciplining back swing of the Perfect Law. The headlines are reading like the pages of the Bible. We see wars and rumors of wars, pestilence, and earthquakes in diverse places. Brothers are turning against brothers, and daughters against their mothers as we look for answers. The answers are not in us. The answers are in He who designed and created all that is.

All the negativity the world is experiencing, as well as any devastation it might experience in the future, has resulted, and will result from the misuse of the Perfect Law. God commissioned the Perfect Law to act positively for the good of mankind. The Perfect Law was designed to give us back what we put out so that we may reap what we sow. The Law stands guard over creation to deliver back upon each of us the positivity we produce by our unselfish, Godly choices. The Law guarantees we receive reward and benefit for all of the good deeds we perform according to His will for us. If we do not know His Perfect Law, or if we know and ignore His Law, making selfish, "unGodly" choices instead, then negative deeds are produced and the Perfect law is enacted to give back to us what we put out. We reap what we have sown.

We can accept our current circumstances as they are being dictated by our past misuse of the Perfect Law, or we can learn the constitution of the Perfect Law and begin to use it as a tool to change our future and turn the tide of history to our favor. Nothing is inevitable as long as man has a free will. According to Godly design, man will choose the way his world will succeed or fail. By our own choices and actions we dictate our own fate and help to decide the future of the world around us.

Chapter 1
The Calling

Advances in civilization have created a busy-ness in our everyday existence that can intercept us and slow us down en route to our God-designed purpose in life. Likewise, this busy-ness can interfere with our relationships, one to another and each to God. We have so much with which to contend every minute of every day. We are the mothers whose minds are enveloped in the macro-family while tending the micro by administrating, cleaning, cooking, chauffeuring, teaching, and whatever else, for both spouse and children. We are the workers whose minds are a virtual spreadsheet, with columns dedicated to the budget, office politics, goal achievement, satisfying bosses, and gratifying clients. We are the students whose minds are scattered between schoolwork, extracurricular commitments, social endeavors, and pleasing the parents, each division of which has subcategories of its own. We would all be better prepared if we would teach juggling skills along with grade school subjects like reading, writing, and arithmetic.

With minds so cluttered and schedules so busy, there is little time left in a day. When do we ever have time for loftier endeavors like understanding and knowing God? One of my very good friends visited me yesterday. When I invited him to a Bible study I was about to commence, he said, "I don't have time for that stuff. Maybe if I could win the lotto I would have more time."

More time? Our calendars allow us 168 hours in a week. If we have not learned to administer those hours while we are poor, having more money will not help. Our problem is not that we need more time. Our problem is we need to better manage the time we do have.

We of the Western Civilizations have immersed ourselves in this crazy, busy-ness we call life. We invented cell phones so we can bring our work to breakfast, lunch, dinner, and home, thus utilizing every possible moment. We invented computers and fax machines and all sorts of automation so that we can crunch our work production to allow ourselves to accomplish more in a twenty-four-hour period. All of this crazy busy-ness keeps us from finding and enjoying life's pleasures. We have only ourselves to blame . . . and Thomas Edison. He invented that darned light bulb that allows us to stay up past dark. God had a design to turn off the lights at a decent hour. In those days before light bulbs, when a man could not see anymore, rather than hurt himself by bumping into things, he retired until daylight.

So, now that it is too late and the light bulb is here, how do we finish all we have to do and still have time for a Bible study? How do we fit God into our schedule? How do we train our children to know Him? Fact is, most of us just do not. There is so little time left in our schedules to allocate toward God and Godly things. Consequently, our personal space and the world around it are deteriorating.

It is an obvious but hard to accept fact that most everything left to itself will deteriorate. Life is designed to wear out. The world is winding down. Eventually, most everything decays or dies, and everything gets worse as it is doing so. History shows us that even great societies, like that of ancient Rome, deteriorate before they desist. Ripe fruit, on or off the vine, decays before it dies, as does every living organism including the human body. Each of us is like a vapor, a breath of air that exists for just a short while and then vanishes away. In our short stay on this Earth, our hope is that we can find love, we can find joy, and we can know peace.

The good news is, we can! God has made a way for us to find love and joy and peace within the tiny space we have been allotted. He did so by preparing the way for each of us to know Him personally and to know He is the Architect and Creator of life and of all created things. He has also made a way for us to enjoin ourselves to Him and His reality so that we can know who we are, where we are going, and what we are supposed to be doing along the way. The down side is that all of this is a process that takes time. If we mismanage our commitments there is little time left to devote to finding and knowing God.

To experience all there is for us to experience, to have all of what has been designed for our betterment, to savor life to the maximum, we must choose to make the connection to God. To enjoy unconditional love, delight in the tranquillity that comes from a peace beyond human understanding, and experience a joy that is unspeakable, mankind must choose to fellowship with the Architect of life, the One Who planned our days and created the environment in which we live. We need to know **Him**, **His** plans, and **His** purposes.

Without God, man cannot experience unconditional love, everlasting joy, and peace beyond human understanding. These are **infinite** attributes of God. Without infinite joy, a man is left with only his own finite, momentary happiness. Without infinite peace, he is left to his own finite coping skills to find comfort. Only God's love is unconditional. Every form of finite love has some qualifier. Secular love, finite love without God, is never unconditional. Without God, man is incomplete.

Without God, and the lessons that teach us about God, there is despair. If apart from God we are unable to find what is necessary to make life complete and maximize our enjoyment of it, then we must retire to be satisfied with what events the circumstances of life dictate. As a result, we can be crushed by life's events. In the world today it is apparent some are beginning to believe this surrender is their only option.

Demoralization is invading our schools, workplaces, televisions, music, and video games. Our newspapers, and our radio and television news programs are evidentiary. There are reports of wars, school shootings at home and abroad, office mates killing one another, and road rage, to name just a few. Hopeless reports are filling our minds and the minds of our children, spouses, friends, and family members with anxiety and/or despair.

The popular answers to the problems of today are self-serving and empty of Godly truth. Instead of offering solutions, our televisions and radios are pumping out secular entertainment in an attempt to ease our pain, while info-mercials, self-help books, and brief news segments born of personal opinions on how to care for or change this-and-that, spit out vacuous and vacillating self-help advice to the many and varied problems facing us. Societal ethics and morals are fading as man attempts to rewrite history and pass laws to remove God from His rightful place in our hearts and as The Sovereign over His creation. Godly wisdom and knowledge are diminishing as we fail to learn spiritual truths for ourselves and fail to pass these truths on to our children.

When I converse with people in today's world, I realize how disgruntled they are becoming. Americans and Europeans alike loathe what they feel is the decay of the old ways when life took its time along a more meaningful and enjoyable pathway. Even young people vocalize anger over their sense of hopelessness. That anger is expressed in their movies, their music, and their video games. It seems everyone is stressed about their future. When I contemplate the circumstances the people of the world must face today versus the days of long ago, I realize how truly blessed I am, and why. God comforts me. Somewhere along the way, God expressed His unconditional love to me or near me. I felt it. I knew it was God, and I latched on to it. God has never let me go.

Exactly when I became fascinated by all things spiritual, I may never know. I know it began in my teens. If we count Aesop's Fables and the Bible stories children hear in Sunday school, it began even before my teens. By age twenty, God had prepared me to receive the enlightenment provided by the scriptures of the Old and New Testaments when I was presented with them. It was then that God sent me an old high school friend, the Reverend James (Jimmy) Marcum, and through him God presented me with my choice to follow Him or continue on the pathway I was traveling. From my own broken awareness, I reached for hope, and God met me at my need. He began opening the scriptures to my understanding because I asked, always giving me more than I expected. Over these past three-and-a-half decades, God has allowed me to see His design for creation. I am still disarmed by the magnificent resplendence of the covenant between God and man and by all of the blessed provisions for man established by our Creator even before time began. I am astounded by the labyrinth of knowledge pressed into a few hundred pages, and the ascendancy of indisputable truth that teases the latent student into the quickening of his spirit. At my first look inside the Bible thirty-five years ago, I was overwhelmed, but I crawled forward like a toddler on his first day in preschool. I read and reread passages and whole books to try to find the meaning in the pages, always seeking, always asking questions. The more I asked, the more God gave me. The more I needed, the more He provided. As I grew in the knowledge of the Lord, I learned the principles of the Kingdom of God and I found benefit from the wisdom these principles offered as I assimilated them into my life.

Over the years I have learned what it means that our Creator is a "living God" with an imperishable commitment to our well being and the well being of all of creation. I have learned the meaning and power of prayer and why petitioning God is paramount to an effective, successful life. I have learned what it means to communicate with God, and I have learned how He communicates with us. Most of all, I have learned to listen to God when He calls. Well, He called yesterday, just after my frenzied friend with his "more time" wish left me. He spoke comforting words into my soul about the days ahead. Then He gave me a mission. He said, "Michael, distill the Biblical message. Make it easier for everyone to understand. Explain to them there is one law, two rules, and a whole bunch of promises. I will take it from there."

I replied (out loud), "Yes Lord." What else am I going to say to the living God who walks among us, and talks with us, who created all there is and could dispose of it all in the twinkle of an eye? His love for mankind is so great, He allowed His only Son to sacrifice Himself and suffer a horrible death so He could deliver us *blameless* to His own doorstep. That sacrifice-for-salvation message has been popular for about two thousand years, but evidently the story is getting tiresome.

As our societies become more secular they are ignoring that same Jesus who, by His sacrifice on the cross, bore away all of the grief we continue to live in by choice.

Does the Architect, our Creator God get upset with us about that? Not really. God knows all things. He knew we would do this, too. He made plans to deal with our latest digression before He ever created the world in which we live. He knew that someday He would be calling upon one of His creations—somebody He had taught to listen early in life, somebody He had made to pay attention—and He would say to him, "Explain to them there is one law, two rules, and a whole bunch of promises."

"God . . . Can you make it any easier for us to find our way to you?"

"NOPE!" came the reply, with mind-imagined reverberation.

Chapter 2

Laws and Rules

This one-law-two-rule message is so simple and so discernable it is inescapable and undisputable. I find it difficult to imagine this message has not been put into a primary study course for use in every school throughout the land, and the world for that matter. This message is about the *cause*. This message explains why every past event in our world occurred the way it did. This message is about how we can change our future and reinvent it to make it work correctly for our own good.

Everything centers around this one simple-to-understand law and the two rules that guide it toward the positive for mankind. This law is instrumental to every aspect of life because this law has implications in our physical world and not just in our spiritual realm. This one law is interconnected in some way to every event in our lives, a connection which drives the necessity to discover its principles and manage it for its benefits. But, first things first.

Ironically, we have to tackle a few definitions in order to identify the attributes and communicate the simplicity of the Perfect Law. The first of these definitions are the words "law" and "rule." The complications of our world caused by the progress and experiences of man during the twentieth century have compounded the more simple meanings of certain common everyday words. Now, many of our words that once had clear and concise definitions have been compromised. Getting back to basics begins first with understanding the language we use to explain those basics.

LAW

What is a law? When I ask that simple question today, our minds might immediately go to the courtroom, demonstrating how confused our world has become. Although I do not intend to discuss jurisprudence, the legal system, or high-tech investigations, our minds go to those places. Our thoughts are held hostage by the experience of Court Television, situation dramas, and daily television news events of high-profile court cases. However, our focus throughout these pages will be on physical and spiritual laws that were in existence long before we had courtrooms.

The basic definition for a law is *that which is laid* (set) *or fixed.* Something set or fixed to its place has permanence. It does not change. Ohm's law of electricity, the laws of aerodynamics, and Newton's law of gravity are examples of some things that are set or fixed and do not change. Many physical and spiritual laws are unfamiliar to many people. In order to convey the definition of a law, we need to use a law that is familiar to most. That last one listed is the best one for our purposes. Everybody has some familiarity with gravity.

We know from experience, what goes up must come down. Gravity works. When we take a spill on the slippery ice in the dead of winter, we remember gravity works! Sometimes we forget the simple laws of life because those laws are always working for us **whether we are conscious of them or not**. That is what makes a law a law.

Spiritual and physical laws are those invisible mandates that we do not have to think about because they are set or fixed, and **they work with or without our knowledge of them**. Thousands of times each day these spiritual and physical laws rule over the events in our lives. Without them, pure chaos would abound.

Laws do what they were designed to do, and they do so with or without our knowledge of them. These are two attributes of the Perfect Law. An attribute is the way something is. A circle is round; water is wet. No one can hand me a square circle or dry water. Wet is what water is. Without wet, water ceases to be water. An attribute is that uniquely obvious trait or defining property of something, that makes it what it is. As we study the Perfect Law, we will be on the hunt for the attributes that define it.

Physical and spiritual laws run our universe. Who devised them, and why are they here? The final chapters of the Book of Job from the **Holy Bible** make it clear that God set all of the laws of our universe into motion during the creation process (Job 38 & 39; Ps 119:89-91). Knowing the selfish free-will choices man would be capable of making, God designed that the physical and spiritual laws of our world would help govern man's choices. God lovingly employed these laws to oversee and to care for all His creations in the event man applied his will in opposition to God's will. To best understand His designs and the purposes behind these laws, we must go back to the Genesis—the beginning.

Laws and Rules 9

THE GENESIS OF THE LAW (studies in Genesis chapters 1-11)

Biblical history records in the book of Genesis that at the very beginning of time God created man in His own likeness (allowing man certain God-like attributes) (Gen. 1:28) and set him as "vice-ruler" by giving man dominion of Earth. In effect, God created the vehicle, set man in the command center, gave him the initiative and the power, and then said, "This is your world to rule and to run in the manner you see fit. I have given you everything you need to accomplish your task. Now, go forth and do it."

By His own invocation, Sovereign God turned the world He had created over to mankind. In His stead, man would be the prime ruler over all of Earth. By the words, *have dominion,* man was free to invent, discover, explore, and put to use all of the elements God had hidden for him in the earth. All of the resources on the ground, in the air, and in the seas were also his to rule. Man was free to employ those resources for his own good pleasure and for the benefit of all those who would follow. Man was to be fruitful, to multiply, and to subdue (Gen. 1:28).

This plan to afford man dominion of the world worked well in the beginning, during the days man spent in the Garden of Eden (Genesis chapters 1-2). At that time, man was still enthralled by God's company in the garden. God's express purposes and designs for all of creation were being heard by man as God communicated them to him while walking and talking with him in that first habitat (Gen 1:28-31; 2:15-25; 3:8-19). However, according to the Bible, at some point after man was dubbed "King of the Earth," he fell from grace. He disobeyed His Creator and took to himself a life apart from God and apart from God's wisdom. (Gen. 3 & 4).

It was man's choice to be other than Godlike. As a result, man was placed outside of the Garden of Eden and separated from God. Although Adam could still return to the edge of the garden to speak with the Voice of God (Genesis 4), man's fellowship and consultations with God were changed. His new nature—his human nature—was his new fixation, not God. Although God had allowed for Adam's repentance and return to the Garden, Adam had no such intentions (Gen. 3:24 says *keep the way of,* and not *to keep man out.*). Adam was enjoying his newfound nature. Adam was in a sense, a god (Isa. 47:10). He had dominion of his world. He could create, discover, explore, and subdue. Adam was free to perform his own good pleasure.

Man had separated himself from advice-on-High and so began working his way through his New World (the world of human reality) using only the finite human endowments gifted to him by his Creator. Without God's counsel, and without God's wisdom and knowledge as a standard, man's gauge of highest and greatest could be elevated to only the level of his own personal best, amplified by his most profound imaginations. Out of necessity, men began listening to one another, developing their *human* knowledge, wisdom, and logic. Adam and his contemporaries soon established their own finite, human perception of the inner workings of the universe. As a result, the philosophy of humanism was born.

Humanism is both an ideal and a religion. Humanism places man as the highest being in the universe, and it negates the existence of or need for an all-encompassing God above him. Consequently, the principle definition of humanism could well be . . . **Other than God**. Adam had a choice: he could choose perfection as designed by Creator-God and live according to *infinite* God's will, or choose instead to follow his own wisdom, a path of discovery and exploration, of trial and error, of human imperfection—the best he could accomplish using his own *finite* human attributes apart from the wisdom and knowledge of God. There were no other choices but these two.

The choice Adam made resulted in mankind's fall from grace into this human reality we now experience. I suggest that after that single decision by Adam, all of mankind's cogitation—every choice and every decision made since—has been, and will continue to be, influenced by one of these two opposing appointments: **God** and **Not-God**. Every religion, philosophy, and ideology alive in our world today chases after one of these two ascriptions.

The cornerstone of all humanistic doctrines solemnized throughout time was laid in place in the days soon after Adam and Eve left the Garden of Eden (Genesis 4). In our day, those humanistic doctrines are the "there is no god" (Not-God) philosophies and secular religions like communism, fascism, socialism, and Darwinism.[1] These are the philosophies and religions that exclude God and replace infinite God with finite man as the highest form of all life. These *"isms"* fall short of God's design for religion, ideology, and philosophy, because after the fall away from God and God's infinite ways and wisdom, man's finite knowledge and wisdom lacked the absolute truth only God can dispense. Most *isms* are concocted of human reason and imaginings and are used to explain how man, by his own human logic and with his broken-off, limited understanding, might comprehend a god to be and his (or her) creations to work.

Humanism, by its very nature, is self serving. Humanism places man in the position of a god (Gen. 2:5). A basic human characteristic or attribute of humankind is self-survival; man is a survivor. It is man's human nature to take care of himself first, to the exclusion of all others. Selfishness is the mode employed to ensure self-survival, and that mode is necessarily one sided toward self.[2] Consequently, **humanism rarely applies itself to the greater good of all** concerned. Rather, it selfishly serves the "save-yourself" self-survival attribute of humankind. The Bible records the consequences of Adam and his contemporaries exploring and utilizing their new found humanism. Within a short period of time after the fall of man, the man who would be king was everyone, and *every imagination of the thoughts of his heart was only evil continually* (Gen. 6:5; Psalm 10:2-11).

Most *isms* in our present day are the end results of Adam and his contemporaries exercising their powers of liberty. *Isms* were established over several millennia as men found similarity in their finite human reasoning and logic and began to agree among themselves as to what would be truth. Neighbors agreeing soon grew into neighborhoods, and those neighborhoods into villages, and then cities, and countries. The people in each community lived together peacefully because together, they agreed upon the truths they had established among themselves, as well as the laws they had created based upon their truths.

Human pseudo-truths established apart from Godly truth are man made, based in finite human logic and reasoning, and serve only those who create them. Every nation, every culture, and every religion throughout the world shares a common set of truths within its own body, but these are not necessarily true to any other body, and neither do they necessarily comply with God's truth. By chapter seven of Genesis, the wickedness of man had grown so that it was necessarily dismantled by a worldwide flood. Still, soon after the memory of the flood began to pass, man reestablished himself on the same course as before the deluge. By the time men began work on Tower of Babel (Genesis 11), man had once again embraced his humanism. This time it surpassed even his own imaginations as they had been expressed before the days of Noah (Gen 11:6).

Although man had fallen from God's reality into his own human reality and was chasing after his finite secular humanism, it was God's design that man should never lose his God-given, God-ordained, **dominion** position as "lord of the Earth." God does not take back His words (Isa 31:2). So, after the fall of man, God allowed man to continue as he was designed: to invent, discover, and explore his world. God's design was that man would see his folly and rise to embrace his Creator once again. Man had no such inclinations, so he continued, wholly on his own, guided only by finite selfish human desire. We can see that man made two choices during his fall away from God. The first was the choice to disobey God's will and purposes, which put man in a state of broken awareness and separated him from God. The second choice man made was just as foolish. He chose to stay in that position (Jer. 2:13-14).

Man liked the idea that he was a god (Gen. 3:5). He liked having dominion power. So onward he went, with little or no direction from God.

I AM / i am

Man had replaced God the I AM, with i am god (Exodus 3:13-14). Without a moral pinnacle on which to base decisions and lacking any Godly-wise principles from on High, man's attitude toward anyone other than himself was subject to only his own understanding of himself as the highest authority in the universe. Every man was king and in possession of what he believed to be the "ultimate truth"—his own. Evil grew in the world as men fought to see which man was **the** king, and who would get to play god.

In spite of man's fall from grace, his mission to go forward was clear. God had designed man to be fruitful and to multiply. He had given man the ability to subdue the earth. Man soon realized he could do all of these things without God's help. He could invent, discover, explore, and create quite well on his own. He could obtain dominion by his own strength, imaginations, and reasoning. It was not necessary to invoke the help of a Creator God. Man had all alone become a god unto himself.

God was not surprised. All of man's endowments and accomplishments were well within God's design and intentions for man from the beginning. Mankind's problems began only after he refused to allow Godliness to play a role in his domination of the world. Instead of choosing to return to God and reenlist Godliness, man chose to worship himself as high ruler of the world, and to worship creation more than the Creator (Romans 1:18-32). Adam had loosed human nature to rule.

Man not only ruled the earth, he dominated it. He conquered the land and divided it as he saw fit, according to his own human standards. Man began using Earth's resources as they pleased little i am. The Biblical record chronicles man's advancements. Without God, every imagination, every thought was evil, and it was only evil continually (Gen. 6:5). That strong statement, so early on in the Bible, showed the power man was capable of employing as little i am (compare Gen. 11:6).

The narrative of the worldwide flood in Genesis tells us that man's evil was equalized by natural means, the result of God's physical laws at work. The weather and a geographical transformation of the Earth produced a year-long flood that spared only a chosen few. That flood cleansed the surface of Earth and readied it for a new beginning.

After the flood, those who survived the cataclysm began to reestablish themselves on the earth. Still, without wisdom from on High, mankind returned to utilizing the resources of the earth to satisfy selfish desire. Supported by more of the same humanistic philosophies, ideologies and religions, mankind's selfish desires once again began to interfere with the purposes of God, and once again it became necessary to interrupt the flow of humanism. God separated great companies of men and women during a single event at Babel by confounding their one language, hence they were unable to understand one another's speech (Genesis 11). I suggest it was at this moment in time that God created our many languages out of one. Those sharing a common language bound together and began to wander from their headquarters at Babel to become the seeds of the different nations of the earth we know today.

Humanism is a sinister agency with an ability to seduce man into thinking he is more than a creation, turning him subtly from his God-designed purpose. More than a creation is a creator or a god. When man believes himself the highest authority or has convinced himself there is no God above him, then he becomes the moral authority and the genius ruler of his world. Everyone else in his world becomes the subordinates that should serve him. His rules are the only rules; what he says and what he does defines the only way life can be in his world.

We cannot know for sure what chaos this Godless agency caused or how that brought about the end of Adam's world so soon after it began. Perhaps by examining a milder, more civilized and controlled destructive process caused by humanism, we can see the capabilities of unrestrained little i am at work. As a model, I suggest we look at the modernization of America, when human progress moved like a plague through nature.

During the eighteenth, nineteenth, and early twentieth centuries we see many of God's creations completely destroyed or displaced by greedy oil magnates, coal magnates, railroad magnates, gold seekers, ranchers, settlers, hunters, trappers, and other self-serving individuals and corporations who cared little about the wake they left in their plunder for happiness, prosperity, and land. Since the fall of man away from God's pure purposes for us, human history has been a witness to millions of examples of the ravaging of our earth and its resources, creatures, and peoples for selfish gain.

For the most part, it would seem man has not been held accountable for the evils he has created, such as war, inhumanities to fellow man, the complacent destruction of other creatures, and the plunder of Earth's natural resources. By allowing man dominance of the earth, God has lain back and established a "hands-off/intervene-by-invitation-only" policy where humans and humanism are concerned. However, Creator God cannot be other than Mother, Father, Provider, and Protector of His creations. These are inseparable attributes of His Divine nature. God has always participated, and will continue to participate in Operation Earth as the overseeing and interacting Lord of the planet (Ex.19:5 Isa 44:24).

God has some very visible and very discernable methods by which He may accomplish His designs without interfering with or intruding upon man's dominion. It was Sovereign God's design that man should be the highest being on Earth (Ps. 8:5; Heb. 2:7) and it was His design to defer to man in every decision made toward the ruling of Earth. Although Sovereign God "tied" His own hands as an active *first-participant* in Earth's events by allowing man his dominion power, any man is free to ask God to help him in any endeavor at any time (Matt. 7:7-8, 21:22, John 16:24). Once asked, God can actively participate as the provider and partner to man, the ruling authority who asked.

Another example of how God can accomplish His designs without direct interaction is found in the physical laws that God created and set into motion to benefit man. These laws are natural equalizers. Two examples here are helpful, the first of which is so simple we often overlook it. Dozens of physical laws are in motion as it rains. These are laws that act with or without God or man actively doing anything to cause them to work. For instance, the rains that fall from the sky gather on the earth and travel on or through the earth to find their way to underground springs and rivers, or overland into our lakes, rivers, and streams. From there, most of that water flows to the oceans where the sun bakes it into steam, sucks pure water back into the clouds, and carries it back over the land to fall again as rain.

All of these actions were designed to be natural equalizers in nature's battle against any harsh effects should man choose to pollute the earth. The rain cleanses the air and the earth, washing the pollutants of man from the sky and from the land into the oceans where they can be swallowed up. The water that carried them there is distilled by the sun into pure water once again and then carried by the winds to wash the land on another day. If man ceased to exist, within a few years the Earth would completely reclaim itself by these natural laws. The earth would once again be pure and clean, pristine like we imagine the Garden of Eden might have been, all the results of God's physical laws. Though we may not see them or understand some of them, physical laws care for Earth every second of every day it is in existence.

There is another facet to how God can accomplish His designs through the physical laws like those that control our weather. God asked Job, *"Hast thou entered into the treasures of the snow? Or hast thou seen the treasures of the hail, **Which I have reserved against the time of trouble, against the day of battle and war?** (Job 38:22-23)"* Most of us would let this verse slip by without a second thought.

Research shows that hail will disrupt even the most sophisticated radar and electronic systems we use on the modern battlefield to guide our weapons and troops. If the balance is not right between a superior nation and a lesser nation that God did not intend to be suppressed, a little adverse weather in the area can equalize the battle and turn it into hand to hand combat. (Any one vice-ruler can request it of God.) It was a change of weather that saved George Washington and his troops when he crossed the Delaware. Heavy weather moved in and hid his troops' movements from the British during the Christmas of 1776, allowing General Washington the upper hand in defeating some British mercenaries at Trenton, New Jersey. That "miraculous" event was a turning point in our revolution for American independence (compare, Ex. 10:21-23).

ABSOLUTE LAW

Physical laws exist, and they rule over us. We do not have to be aware of them or understand them to make them work. These laws work whether or not we think about them, and they work in spite of what we do think about them. No one has to get up early to turn on gravity. There is no switch that turns on or off any of our physical laws for the day. Nor does God have a guru hidden away in the Himalayan Mountains who rises at four in the morning to pray, "Oh God, our God, please let gravity work for the world today." A law does not have to be invoked by prayer, understood by man, or necessarily applied to the need. Laws were set into motion by the Creator of all things at the very beginning of time, and each one works incessantly to do the job it was designed to do apart from any interaction by man.

Now it is a good thing that gravity works. Not that it makes any difference, but I think God did a really fine job designing gravity the way He did. God could have made gravity differently. He could have arranged it so that everything would fall up, and then make all of his creatures with lead feet. It would never rain, but then we would not need the cleansing effects of rain if the paper we throw away falls up into outer space. No matter, God chose to make gravity work the way it does, and gravity became a law.

Whether or not you choose to believe in the law of gravity makes no difference to the law; gravity will continue to work anyway. **Laws are absolute**, and because they are absolute, we can depend on them to do the job they were designed to do. Laws do absolutely what they were designed to do **no matter how, or what, or even if we think about them**. Laws were designed to work that way. If we had to remember to make gravity work for ourselves, most of us would float away in our sleep. Gravity is a law, it is absolute, and it works. It is not yes on Sundays, and no on Wednesdays. It is not positive for you, and negative for me. There are no grey areas to a law. (2 Cor. 1:19-20) It is what it is, and it does what it does, and like God, it does not change (Mal 3:6, James 1:17, Is 31:2). If you were standing on the edge of a cliff that dropped straight down 1500 feet, and you chose not to believe in gravity, your first step forward would be what those of us remaining alive would call *thinning the herd*. Gravity works! Those who choose to believe benefit from believing. Those who do not will reap the consequences.

Knowing that a law does work—and that it works absolutely—allows us to use it to our advantage. This is another very important concept to grasp, and it is this truth that allows us to use the Perfect Law as a tool for our own good. Although a law does not *have* to be invoked by prayer, understood by man, or applied to the need, a law *can* be invoked by prayer, understood by man, and applied to a need if man chooses to do so. For instance, we can understand the law of gravity and apply it to create roller coasters for our enjoyment or gravity driven mechanical presses to produce our manufactured goods.

When gravity got in our way, we studied the birds and discovered the laws of aerodynamics. We found that when wind passes over a curved wing, the pressure above the wing is not as great as the pressure below the wing, causing the wing to lift. Then we invented the airplane, and every day we pretend to defy the law of gravity that once was in our way. I say "pretend" because gravity still works. Consequently, when an invention that opposes gravity fails, like an airplane, well . . . a law is a law. It is absolute, and it works.

UNIVERSAL LAW

Laws are both universal and transcendent. A law is universal because it is found everywhere. Gravity has existed everywhere in our world during every generation since the beginning of time. A law is transcendent because, no matter the station, it does not change. Gravity does not change as it reaches across every culture, social boundary, race, religion, border, politic, science and philosophy in the world. The law of gravity works on the football field and in the classroom. It works in outer space and on the job site. It has always worked and will always work in these places and in all places because laws are universal and transcendent.

A law performs according to design. Laws do not think, rationalize, or despair. Laws have no passion or prejudice. They work without empathy or emotion to perform the task for which they were created.

The law of gravity does not care that you are white or red, blonde haired or brown eyed, Christian or Buddhist. Laws perform absolutely, transcendently, and universally according to design, without passion or prejudice.

RULES

In the explanation of a law, we defined the attributes of a law as absolute, universal, transcendent, and as operating without passion or prejudice. It has been explained that should we choose to ignore or defy a law, there are consequences that may be immediate and devastating. It is not so with a rule. Rules are more like suggestions. We can take them or leave them. Rules, unlike laws, may be disregarded. They were not made to be disregarded, but they can be. Unlike a law, a rule can be misinterpreted, abused or ignored. Because defying or denying a law can have immediate and devastating consequences, we protect ourselves by establishing rules. **A rule is defined as a prescribed, suggested, or self imposed guide for conduct or action.** We might say a rule is an advisor for our protection. Rules protect us from becoming prey to laws.

We can use the same 1500 foot cliff we used to define a law to help us define a rule. The punishment for disobeying the law of gravity lives only an inch over the edge of that steep cliff and provides disaster for any transgressors of that law. A rule created to advise or protect us against falling into the hands of that law is a sign post stuck firmly in the ground at the edge of that cliff that says, "Do not walk beyond this point." Such a rule has no power and is nothing more than a suggestion to protect us from the consequences of a law. Rules designed to protect us were not made to be ignored, but they can be. If this rule is disregarded, the one who opposes the rule may have to deal with the consequences of the law just beyond it.

We may defy a rule and get away with it. That is the difference between a law and a rule. For instance, we may jump from the cliff, grab that signpost on the way down, and pull ourselves back up. In such an instance, we are defying only the rule and not the law. We know the law will do us harm if we do not grab onto something and pull ourselves back to safety. We are merely testing the rule to see if it can be stretched. Holding the signpost as we jump, grabbing it after we jump, grabbing it near the top, or at the last possible moment, grabbing it near the bottom, are different ways of testing how far we can stretch that rule.

Many of the laws in the Bible are actually rules. Take for example, the Ten Commandments (Exodus 20). Pick one, any one, like Commandment #6: *Thou shalt not kill.* Commandment #6 is just a rule. Some people do disregard that rule and appear to get away with murder in some instances. Disregarding a rule can have immediate and certain consequences on the earth, but not always. If the person who ignored the rule *thou shalt not kill* is caught, he will have to deal with the consequences of the laws at the end of that rule. In the case of murder, the primary consequence to be dealt with afterwards would be dictated by the law-of-the-land in which the murder was committed. The secondary but more formidable consequences that must be dealt with are dictated by God's spiritual laws.

NOTES

1. I chose to list Darwinism as a religion or philosophy rather than a science because it is unproven. Evolution, like Creation is a faith-based ideology. The proponents of the Darwinian religion have faith that someday they will find an example of the "missing link" to prove their conjectures. There is much more evidence to the contrary. Many books reporting the conflict have been written by qualified scientists to debunk the claims of evolution theorists. See *Evolution—the Fossils Say No*, by Dr. Dwaine T. Gish

2. Selfishness and self-survival are not wrong, bad, or evil. These are primal attributes of humankind. We are spiritual beings experiencing a temporary, human existence. While our eternal spirit is visiting this physical dimension we call life, our physical body is its temporal habitat. Our soul, that intangible part of us that was created when our eternal spirit joined itself to our physical body, is very protective of our mortal self. Our soul is where choice lives; in our soul is our free-will to think, do, and be what we desire. Our soul knows that if our physical body dies, our eternal spirit will have no "house" or temple to live in on this physical side of life and must return to God in the eternal. Consequently, our soul will do anything and everything it can to sustain our body and ensure its functions.

When a soul is not tempered by spiritual wisdom and knowledge, or when the soul quenches the positive leading of the spirit and follows the lusts of the flesh instead, our human nature can go awry causing chaos. Such chaotic instances give humankind reason to equate wrong, bad, or evil with selfishness although selfishness is nothing more than a primal attribute of humankind that we may choose to employ for good or evil.

Chapter 3

Spiritual Law

In addition to God's physical laws that guide our tangible earthly substances there is another set of God-designed, God-initiated laws. These are known as spiritual laws. Spiritual laws can be explained as those invisible, mysterious set of mandates that guide the intangible universe we cannot see. Some examples of these spiritual laws are *The fear of the Lord is the beginning of knowledge* (Prov. 1:7; 26-29; 2:3-5), and *The fear of the Lord is the beginning of wisdom* (Ps. 111:10; Prov. 9:10-11). Fear is a respectful reverence of God that comes from knowing God *is* (Heb. 11:6-7). These two spiritual laws tell us our respectful reverence of God will guarantee that His knowledge and wisdom will become our knowledge and wisdom. Another example of a spiritual law is *Charity never faileth,* or better yet, UNCONDITIONAL LOVE NEVER FAILS (Jer. 31:3; 1 Cor. 13:8). This law of love is self-explanatory.

Spiritual laws are intangible laws that touch and affect the invisible, moral, and spiritual sides of our beings. The greatest spiritual law is the one just mentioned—**The Law of Love**. The second most important spiritual law is the **Perfect Law of Liberty**. This is the law that stands guard over all of creation to ensure Godly design prevails.

This law is the ultimate, equalizing force of God, designed by Him to be the one just instrument by which fairness and justice are measured out upon all of creation. Ultimately it is this law that has guided, provisioned, adjusted, and leveled every element of creation since the beginning and will continue to do so until God's design for Earth is finished. So perfect is this law, so much is it in control, so Godly is its design, that because of this one law, **we can be asssured that life on Earth was designed to be perfectly fair for everyone.** As anyone who acknowledges the infinite perfection of God might assume, God has made provision for life to be completely just and perfectly fair for every human being.

Life was designed by God to be ideal, and part of that ideal is that life is fair to all. **Fairness is an attribute of life.** God hammered this attribute of life home with a spiritual law that says, . . . *God is faithful, who will not suffer you to be tempted above that ye are* able. He added that He *will with the temptation also make a way to escape, that ye may be able to bear it* (1 Cor. 10:13). God plainly says you will never be caught in a temptation that is larger than your ability to remove yourself from it. After all, *with God all things are possible* (Matt. 19:26b). *In all these things we are more than conquerors, through him that loved us* (Romans 8:37). We are victors! Man's conception, or better yet, his humanistic excuse for the failures in his selfish existence, is that life is *so unfair*. This concept ignores God's love, provisions, and protection for His creations. The idea that life is unfair is an example of pure humanism at its finest. Ignoring God to behave selfishly, and then blaming any failure caused by our selfishness on anything other than self, is pure humanism!

Life is fair, and it is fair for everyone. It might not appear that way when we take our eyes off of God to concentrate instead on the reports of the news media, but life being fair for everyone was and is the intention of God (Job 34:10-12; Ps. 68:19). Just because man is bothered by war, starvation, and disease does not mean that God designed and intended these. Flaws, like those of war, starvation, and disease, are in God's knowledge and design only by the injection of humanism. God gave man dominion of the earth, and man chose to ignore the infinite wisdom and knowledge of God to chase after his own finite, selfish desires instead. Not being attentive to God's design and purposes for Earth and mankind, resulted in the humanistic doctrines that spur wars, starvation, disease, and all the other negatives that cause despair in the hearts of men.

The Perfect Law is the statute designed and ordained by God to guarantee life will be fair for everyone. In order to deliver fairness and equality, this one perfect law oversees and has the power to supersede all other laws except for the Law of Love. It even overrides and overrules nature. The Perfect Law is the law that keeps the needle pointing straight and ultimately makes all things right. That includes returning to balance any portion of life that is out of balance.

How does the Perfect Law accomplish its goal of making life fair for all? It is this law that is employed by God to sit in judgement over the finished works of men and the actions that caused them. The Perfect Law has a peculiar interaction with the deeds or finished works of every free will choice made by man. The Perfect Law "reads" the deed, interprets the intent, and then returns the deed to the doer with the same intent.

The Perfect Law was set into motion to give back with interest

Spiritual Law

everything that is put out. The Perfect Law was designed to reward our Godliness. Godliness is a part of that likeness to God that man received during creation (Gen. 1:26). By the Perfect Law, God can continuously bless us as we chase after Him, His way, and His design. According to God's design, life can only get better; the Perfect Law will see to it.

By the Power of the Perfect law, if a man performs a good deed, a good deed will be returned to him. If he performs an evil or selfish deed, an evil or selfish deed will come back upon him. The Perfect Law is like a judge that juries and levies equitable and impartial verdicts to both the just and the unjust, to the workers of good and the workers of evil. This law then delivers reward or punishment according to those verdicts and does so without partiality. The Perfect Law acts as judge, jury, and executor to ensure creation stays on a course toward Godliness and away from evil.[1]

God by Sovereign invocation has determined to stand down as an interactive, first-participant in the events of man. He has determined man will have dominion of Earth. Therefore, God will do nothing unless he does it by invitation through a man. Someone must ask Him.

To protect all of creation against the selfishness of man, God designed and enacted an overseeing law, the Perfect Law, making man responsible to himself for the free-will choices he was designed and permitted to make. This law views man's deeds and intents and equalizes them by giving back what was put out. Knowledge of the Perfect Law causes man to think, plan, choose wisely, and treat other creations as he himself would want to be treated. As a result, God is relieved of the business of adjudicating creation. God is free to fulfill His desired commitment toward creation, which is to shower creation with unconditional love.

The Perfect Law acts on God's behalf to guide mankind in the paths of righteousness, and this law will return man to that path should he stray. It is the innate knowledge of this law in our spirit that causes every self-willed being to be rational, conscionable, and to care for his fellow man (and all of creation around him) as he would care for himself. Man knows innately that what he does to and for others will come back to him.

The Perfect Law, like all laws, is universal and transcendent. It reaches across every border and has done so since the beginning of time. Its design cannot be bettered. It is a perfect law, a law nearly forgotten, shelved with the myths and folklore of history. The Perfect Law is the Law God would have us take from those shelves and bring into the spotlight at this time to enlighten a world that needs an adjustment. Although this world seems driven by media and by "Not-God" social madness, the majority of the people on Earth are Godly people from all walks of life, people who are innately aware of God and Godliness (Romans 2:7, 10-13). This is their time. This is their day.

This time in our history is about taking dominion control, and assuring God's design for the earth is put in place by removing the designs of the Not-God constructionists. This day in which we live is the end of an era, the end of a time. The "end times," mentioned often in the Bible, do not designate the end of the world. The end of times mentioned were meant to announce an end to *this way of doing things*. An example of the end of an era or of an end of times would be the coming of Jesus. His birth, death, and resurrection put an end to *the old Hebrew ways of doing things*. Jesus was the *lamb of God* and the final sacrifice in a long history of sacrifice. When He declared *It is finished* (John 19:30), He was telling us the end of a long era was over. Life by law had passed away, and life by love would became the *new way of doing things*.

A cursory look at the subjects of the books on the "best seller" list in any of our bookstores will reveal that once again we may be about to enter into such a time in Earth's history. Those subjects reveal that man is being touched by the Spirit of God today. It is as if God is calling us to make the necessary changes so that we can move on from this era into *a new way of doing things*. I suggest He has prepared that way by allowing the knowledge of the Perfect Law to come into the spotlight in the final hours of this way of doing things. The Spirit of God and the Perfect Law working together will guide the hearts of men to where our future will be.

The Perfect law is a Jewish law, a Christian law, an Islamic law, a Hindu law, a Buddhist law, a pagan law, a moral law, an historic law, a scientific law, and more. I do not profess an ability to teach it from all of these views as I am not versed in all of these genres. However, I can and will teach it from the perspective in which I am well versed, Judeo-Christian history as it is recorded in the Holy Bible. I expect others who are more expertly educated than myself, to report it from their own persuasions as they come to understand the constitution of the Perfect Law.

This is the ultimate law, the Perfect Law. This is the one law known among the worshipers of every major religion, and it is known by those who have never known a religion. The Perfect Law is the one law that is familiar to every person because it is innate in the spirit of every one of us. We are each born with the spiritual knowledge of this law and how it works. It is part of our self-survival package and is as intrinsic to our spirit as eating or breathing is to our physical bodies. Although the physical side of our human nature defaults to self survival, our spiritual consciousness defaults to the Perfect Law and causes us to be rational and conscionable toward the rest of creation, in spite of our selfish human-predisposition.

Consider that if we neglect to follow an architect's design for a building, eventually that building will fail, in part or overall. Because God is The Architect of our world, when we neglect to follow his plans for this world as we direct it and rule over it from our dominion, eventually some part of our alternative choice will fail. **Every one of the problems or solutions in our world today is a direct or indirect result of the Perfect Law God set into motion to oversee His design for our world,** a design from which we have strayed. How men, governments, and nations have been punished or delivered, blinded or guided, blessed or cursed, elevated or brought down, can all be explained by the Perfect Law. As we study the Perfect Law from these pages, we will realize how familiar this law is to us. *What goes around comes around* is common knowledge, both in principle and in experience. I am merely retelling a familiar story using the long history of men who came before. I am using the Bible to enlighten or perhaps expand our knowledge of this law that we already know exists to guide our life and the lives of everyone around us. My hope is to help us all learn to use this law as a tool for success, which is what it was designed by God to be.

NOTES

1. The idea of a deed returned for each deed put forth was not designed to put man into bondage or lay a burden upon him that is more than he can bear. The Perfect Law was put in place to make man responsible for his choices and his actions. Knowledge of the Law provides incentive for the doing of good.

A deed put forth may not necessarily be returned exactly the same way. If we give ten dollars toward a charity, we might receive a free vacation in return. If we steal somebody's car, our house might burn down. As we explore the constitution of the Perfect Law we shall see the law provides only that we gain or loose the same or more than we put out.

The Perfect Law is in place to make us consciously aware of our actions and our thoughts so that we might think and rethink, plan and organize the events of our day to avoid suffering, and advance Godliness. Everyone of our decisions and actions are weighed in the balance of the Perfect Law. Flipping a light switch is a benign deed. What is returned is light. Saying I love you, thanking God for the squirrel in your front yard, and the food on your table are positive deeds that will be returned as positive deeds or be used to undo three negative deeds should you make three negative choices in your day. Most of us end our day on a positive note with positive actions and deeds weighing in on the scale of the Perfect Law. Our positive days are pushed forward to the next and build for our future.

Chapter 4
Understanding the Bible as History

If you are unfamiliar with or have had a negative experience with the Bible, do not be turned away because I have chosen the Bible as a source to guide us in the understanding of the Perfect Law. The purpose of this book is not to convert or convict or proselytize, but rather to counsel in the understanding of this law and how it rules over us. We need not be Christian or even religious to understand that the Perfect Law does work.

For this study, I am interested primarily in focusing on the recorded history set forth by the Bible. For the most part, this study could be subtitled, **the Perfect Law as it is Understood from the History of the Bible**. I chose the Bible because I have spent the greater portion of my life studying its pages. The Bible has become more familiar to me than any other history book, and so it is my history book of choice to demonstrate the importance the Perfect Law plays in our reality. Someone could just as easily use American history or mechanical physics to explain this law because the Perfect Law is universal and transcendent.

The Bible is first and foremost a history book, a recording of four thousand years of events by numerous authors, assembled over a period of approximately fifteen hundred years. It is the saga of a single Hebrew family throughout all of its generations. It tells their stories and the stories of those whose lives they touched. This history book also records the wisdom lessons man has come to understand during those four millennia. As a history book filled with wisdom, it serves most readers much like a religious *Farmer's Almanac*. I have offered references to chapters and verses from this religious almanac (the **King James Version**). These are suggested to highlight the history and wisdom recorded in antiquity relative to the lesson.

Because it is about a Hebrew family and their history from their beginnings through Judaism to Christianity, the Bible is one-sided in favor of the Judeo-Christian philosophy, just as mechanical physics is one-sided toward science. Try to put the religious aspects aside in order to get to the heart of this message. The Perfect Law that the Bible presents is also the Perfect Law that arbitrates science as well as the Perfect Law that arbitrates politics. The Perfect Law is **not** one-sided toward Christianity; it is universal and transcends all boundaries including those that are spiritual. The Perfect Law is designed to be employed as a tool by any and all who know it and understand it, no matter their religious or nonreligious persuasion. These pages merely use the history of the Bible to tell the story of the Perfect Law. This law, and the two rules that guide it foremost, are all we need to find love, happiness, and prosperity in this life. All of the evidence for this can be found among the pages of the Bible and the history recorded therein. I have labored to condense that evidence into the few pages of this book with the hope of inspiring readers into a perpetual study of their own through the persuasion of their choosing. Having said all of that, allow me to rewrite the first paragraph of this chapter so you can read it as it was intended. The next paragraph is that rewrite. I have removed all religious aspects and left only the historical in place. By this, the bias created by the word Bible will be more evident.

If you are unfamiliar with the history of man, or have had a bad experience, never having found a history book worth reading, do not be turned away because I have chosen history as a source to guide us in the understanding of the Perfect Law. My intention, by using the subject of history, is not to convert you into a history buff or convict you so you feel you must read history, but rather to use history to counsel you in the understanding of the this Law and how it rules over us all. We need not be historians or even own a history book to understand that the Perfect Law does work.

PERFECT INTERPRETATION

The Bible is not only a history book, it is an inspirational book. The history recorded in it reflects a relationship between God and man. That relationship acknowledges God as the author of the scriptures. Although written by men, the words were inspired by God (Hebrews 1:1-2).

Our challenge, is to try to understand the words of the scriptures as they were inspired to be understood. If God is perfect and He authored the words of the Bible, then the words should not contradict one another. They should flow into the single story God wanted us to know.

Imagine the entire conglomerate of sixty-six books that make up the

Bible is one long, straight board and each verse of the Bible is a sewing needle. When we comprehend a verse of the Bible as God intended it, we can pound the needle that represents that verse into that board somewhere. When we understand every verse as **God intended** (Ps. 33:4), all of the needles should be in the board. If we are correct in our interpretation **as God, the Author, would have it be known,** we should be able to look through the eye of the first needle and see right through the center of every eye of all the other needles. That would be perfect as God is perfect. If one needle is out of alignment, it is not necessarily because someone made an error in translation. Even if it were, God knows those mistranslations and is able to show us what He intended instead. I suggest that any misunderstanding that might arise from a proper translation of the Bible comes because we have misinterpreted or failed altogether to hear God's intentions for the interpretation.

IMPERFECT INTERPRETATION

"... *I am the LORD which exercise loving-kindness,* **judgement,** *and righteousness, in the earth: for in these things I delight, saith the LORD."* Jeremiah 9:24b

"For the LORD is our **judge***, the Lord is our lawgiver, ..."* Isaiah 33:22a

"Now will I shortly pour out my fury upon thee: and **I will judge** *thee according to thy ways, and will recompense thee for all thine abominations."* Ezekiel 7:8

"For the Father (God) **judgeth** *no man; ..."* John 5:22a (Jesus Speaking)

"Also unto thee, O Lord, belongeth mercy: for thou renderest to every man according to his work." Psalm 62:12

What contradiction! God judges, but He does not judge, yet He renders judgement. Is God authoring confusion? First Corinthians 14:33 clearly states God does not author confusion. Therefore we must realize that, somehow, all of these verses have to work together and must agree with one another in a logical way. If there can be no confusion in what God authors, then there must be an answer to how all this contradiction can be but one single thought that is true.

There is always an answer to every question concerning the Bible. If we want to know the answers, God is the one who provides them. It does not come from Bible commentaries or opinions, but by asking God and through silence in prayer as we listen for His answer (Ps. 119:18). It comes also through an abundance of serious Bible study, as opposed to "Bible diving;" a phrase not unlike the expression "dumpster diving," which is the act of diving into trash dumpsters to find usable trash. Let us coin the phrase "Bible diving," and define it as the act of going to the Bible to find that for which we are looking, instead of that which God would have us to know.

Imperfect interpretations of the Bible can cause contradictions between Bible scriptures. There are mainly three causes for any discrepancy in the Bible record. All three are related in some way to misinterpretation.

CONTROVERSY

To begin, the Bible is two books in one. I am not speaking here of the two testaments, nor am I singling out any of the sixty-six individual books that make up the King James Version of the Bible. I consider both testaments and all of the books combined to be one single manuscript. I hope to impart that within the one manuscript, there are two distinctly different books. The first book is the historical record of God's **intentions** for man. The second book is the historical record of what man did with God's intentions.

Portions of the first book are sometimes cryptic. This can occasionally cause problems in interpretation, which in turn can make portions of the Bible appear contradictory. Misinterpretations because of cryptic language is the least cause behind Bible contradiction. God is not purposely making Himself unavailable, nor is He trying to hide Himself from any of us. God is available to all who choose to seek after Him (John 3:16; Rom. 10:13), but there are portions of God's message to us that need to be spiritually discerned and not available to every eye. These mysteries are hidden from those who would do harm to the Kingdom of God, but are designed to be understood by those who have ears to hear and eyes to see. One fine example of why portions of the Bible might be cryptic can be found in 1 Corinthians 2:6-16: *Howbeit, we speak wisdom among them that are perfect: yet not the wisdom of this world, nor of the princes of this world, that come to nought: But we speak the wisdom of God in a mystery, even the hidden wisdom which God ordained before the world unto our glory; Which none of the princes of this world knew: for had they known it, they would not have crucified the Lord of Glory. But as it is written, Eye hath not seen, nor ear heard, neither have entered into the heart of man, the things which God hath prepared for them that love him. But God hath revealed them unto us by his Spirit; for the Spirit searcheth all things, yea, the deep things of God. For what man knoweth the things of a man, save the spirit of man which is in him? Even so the things of God knoweth no man, but the Spirit of God. Now we have received, not the spirit of the world, but the Spirit which is of God; that we might know*

Understanding the Bible as History

the things that are freely given to us of God. Which things also we speak, not in the words which man's wisdom teacheth, but which the Holy Ghost teacheth; comparing spiritual things with spiritual. But the natural man receiveth not the things of the Spirit of God: for they are foolishness unto him: neither can he know them, because they are spiritually discerned. For who hath known the mind of the Lord, that he may instruct him? But we have the mind of Christ.

For the most part, God's intentions for man are right up front and plainly recorded. Even God's "hidden" messages, though shrouded in mystery, are available to any who desire to search them out. (Prov. 2:1-4; Jer. 29:13; Matt. 11:15; Matt. 13:11). The mysteries remain hidden only to those who have been deluded by the Kosmos[1] system and the prince who rules it (2 Cor 4:3-4). Cryptic messages are a minor cause of Bible contradiction.

A second and more notable cause of Biblical contradiction is the dichotomy[2] of the scriptures. The Bible is two books, and those two books are mutually exclusive reports that are opposed by contradiction. The Bible contains the written records of the history of man from two points of view. One view of the Bible is as God intended history to be by design and how God intended His design to be carried out by man. The other view is how man, in his fallen state of consciousness, perceived God's design and how he then staged his perception and recorded that history. The difference between these two contrasting histories (what God designed, and what fallen man did with God's design) is dichotomous. The second cause of Bible contradiction is this dichotomy, the recorded contest between what God wanted for man, and what man selfishly desired and produced instead.

It is important that we understand mysteries and dichotomies in the Bible and that we learn how to recognize them and decipher them because we do not want to confuse them with the third and more pervasive reason we have Bible contradiction.

The leading cause of Bible contradiction is the result of misinterpretation (not mistranslation). Misinterpretation is most often produced by ignorance, but it can also be manufactured by those who would do harm to the Kingdom of God. Humanism is sinister. In order for a humanist to dominate and find a position as a god on earth, he must refute the position of Sovereign God. What better way to do this than to confuse those who are looking for spiritual truth and make them believe that the Bible, the primary book that explains how one can know God, is a lie and full of contradiction. These Kosmos deluded people search for ways to put God aside to enable their Not-God constructs. They will go to any lengths to remove the Bible and its religion from prominence. They will do anything and everything necessary to displace Godly ethics and morals. They are compelled by their desire to be a god, to drive a wedge between man and everything Holy.

The ongoing story of Romans, chapter 1, verses 18-32 exposes the purpose behind the reconstruction of scripture by Not-God people. Likewise, religionists who cannot or choose not to live according to Godly design may also reconstruct scripture to benefit their self-indulgence. For example, I might have a hidden, sinful indulgence, and though I go to church every week, I refuse to repent. If I am hiding my iniquities that keep me from experiencing the gifts of God, like healing and faith, then I might extract and reassemble certain scriptures from the Bible to say these gifts no longer exist; these gifts died along with the Apostles. Now I have an excuse why I am sick all of the time and why I cannot pray for your health with results, even though the real cause is my hidden sin. Such practices are no less than the same humanism practiced by those who altogether refuse to acknowledge God.

Misinterpretation, the third and most pervasive cause of Bible contradiction, can also be initiated by well-meaning, hard-working Christians who misunderstand, thus misinterpret, the Bible. Those in positions to teach often do not take the time to perfect their knowledge and know God. Instead, they lean to Bible commentary and/or their own understanding to assemble their Bible lessons (Prov. 3:5). Once these teaching deeds are released into our physical reality, it is near impossible to undo them. Did you know the number "three" is mentioned nowhere in the Bible with reference to the number of wise men visiting Mary and Joseph at the birth of Jesus? We have no idea how many wise men there were. Nor are we sure that December 25th is the date of Jesus' birth. Once again, there is no Biblical mention. However, the fact that shepherds were grazing their sheep speaks more to a late spring or early summer nativity (Luke 2:8). And if we study the chronological record, Jesus could have been nearly two years old when the wise men visited Him. All of these facts are well known, but changing the traditional Bible story of three wise men bearing gifts to a baby wrapped in swaddling clothing and lying in a manger on Christmas day would be very difficult to do.

ALL-KNOWING GOD

Natural man (man operating out of his own human nature) has a limited understanding of God. Having been broken off and separated from the wisdom of God, natural man can only interpret God and the actions of God based on his own imagination and experiences, and those of others like himself. Consequently, his perception of God is mired. His ability to comprehend truth as God explicates truth has likewise been compromised, distorted by his fallen nature, and coerced by evil. Separated from God unto his own humanism, man can no longer see, interpret, or understand the bigger picture. Man, without God's help, is incapable of comprehending the fullness of God. If man does not seek to know God, he will only understand the parts of that picture that are relative to his fallen state of consciousness. If man acknowledges a god from that broken state of awareness, he imagines that god to be somewhat like himself—a man, but somehow more—perhaps a superman—a man like himself, only better, bigger, and with increased power.

After the fall of man away from God, any true concept of God became unimaginable to man (Isa. 46:5,9). The infinite is little understood by the finite. If God were to speak to us and explain Himself using only His own voice, we might hear words like *uhoiasd oq ooihk j,* spoken as an ocean or the wind might speak them, totally incomprehensible to anything in man's relativity. Our grandest, finite understanding of God is so very incomplete. If God were an ocean, man's highest concept of Him would not fill even one drop of water in that ocean (Isa 55:8-9). Let us explore this idea.

If we isolate just one of the attributes of God, we can undertake to explore it to its depths in a man-to-God comparison. Perhaps by this exercise we will see how little we really do know and comprehend of infinite God. For this exercise, I have chosen God's all-knowing attribute of omniscience (1Sam 2:3). Let us begin.

We have knowledge. We can apply ourselves to understanding and grow to know many things, such that we could say, "We have great knowledge," or "We have a lot of knowledge." We could begin buying up all of the libraries and universities where knowledge is stored and taught such that we can say, "Now we have a great deal of knowledge, and knowledge is in our hand." We can buy up every book, magazine, and paper ever written, but when we come to the end of our learning and collecting of all knowledge, the best we can ever say is, "We **have** all knowledge."

God, on the other hand, does not **have** knowledge; He **is** knowledge. God does not **have** anything; He is everything. God is all things (Eph.1:23) , and God is knowledge (1 Cor 15:28). This is not to be confused with the philosophy of Pantheism wherein exists the idea that all things corporately are God. The "All" of God cannot be contained in "things." *The heavens and the highest heavens cannot contain Him* (1Kings 8:27; 2Chron. 2:6,6:18). God is above all things. He is bigger than all things corporately. Travel as far as you can travel into outer space, to the very ends of the heavens, and you will find that God is just beginning (Ps 139:7-12, Acts 17:24-28).

The idea that God is all things is akin to saying God is omnipresent or everywhere present (Jer. 23:24). There is no place where God is not, which makes him a practical part of everything that is (Eph 1:22). God is in every atom of the universe (Col. 1:17). Ideologically, creation is a part of the fabric of God. Creation is the skin of God, so to speak. However, creation itself, even as a whole, is not God any more than our bodies are us.

We see another perspective if we say we **have** things, because God **is** all things (1 Cor 15:28). For instance, I **have** love. God **is** love. I have love **because** God is love. If God were not love, then my having love would give me something of which God was unaware. Unaware God, without something I possess, is not complete God. Because I have it and He does not, I would be better than God, greater than God. That is pure foolishness. Anything man possesses, tangible or intangible, he has because God is that. We have only because He is. There is nothing new (Eccl. 1:9).

The moon has no light of its own, yet it lights our nights here on earth. The moon merely reflects the light of the sun. The moon **has** light because the sun **is** light, *and the moon is in a position to reflect that light.*

Likewise, when we experience something, we can be assured it is only a reflection of some facet of who or what God is. There is no new thing under the sun (Eccl. 1:9). If I can reason, it is because God is logic. If I can feel, it is because God is sensation. If I can praise, it is because God is worship (Compare Rom.13:1-3).

Let us remain focused on knowledge. Perhaps we can gain a sense of what it means **to be** knowledge, versus to **have** knowledge. We know God is smart, wise, intelligent, logical, rational, and sensible. Our imagination says all of that has to be multiplied by infinity because He is God. Infinity, like God, is another concept that can only be imagined by man. As a finite being, we cannot comprehend what infinity might be.

We give our understanding of God's knowledge a name . . . **omniscience**. God is omniscient, or all knowing. But what does that really mean? In part, that means God knows everything we are thinking right now (1Chron 28:9). But it also means He knows everything we have ever thought and everything we will ever think. It also means He knows that about our mothers, our friends, and every other person who is alive now, has ever lived, or will live in the future. Already we cannot comprehend how much knowledge that is, but it is still on a scope that is manageable; that is, we can still imagine how much knowledge that might be.

Add to that, *God knows **every** thought we are not thinking at this moment . . .*

Now, stop! Read that last sentence again. Close your eyes and meditate on the concept for a moment.

At this moment, we are thinking a singular thought directed by what we are reading, but God knows the quad-zillions of thoughts each of us is capable of thinking, but are not thinking right now. Along with everything we are thinking right now, God knows all the things we should have, could have, and would have thought, but did not, as well as all of the things we can, might, and should think, but will not (Ps139:1-6). And He knows that about every person, who ever was, is now, or will be. And He knows that about every person who could have been, but is not, those that should be, but are not, and those who might, but will not be. All of that stretches across time as well, as if to say, "What if Adam or Eve were to mate with the child you and Elvis never had? What are all of the things that person would never think?" God knows that too (Job 42:2 Ps 147:5, Isa. 46:9-10). The brain initiates a meltdown when we hit a point beyond imagination. The concept of this much knowledge is no longer even imaginable to the finite human mind. It is just confusion. Still we have not filled up the drop of water in the ocean of this one facet of God we are calling omniscience. There is more.

God knows every blade of grass that is, was, will be, could have been, should be, or might be. He knows every hair on our head, that ever was, is, or will be, and that is a momentary counting for some of us. He knows every bird, every feather on every bird, every louse on every feather, every cell in every louse, every molecule in every cell, every atom in every molecule, every quark in every atom that ever was, is now, will be, was not, is not now . . . How huge is a knowledge that knows what the difference would be in each atom of our world, should a single proton or pulsar or even a quark move from one atom to the next until that single unit of energy had visited and engaged with every other atom that ever did or did not, could or could not, should or should not exist? You get the idea. How can man even conceive the knowledge of someone like God, let alone conceive the whole of God Himself? Having a melt down? Well, we are not finished yet.

Herein we have just been considering what God knows of our world. Let us not discount all of the other worlds that might, could, should, are, were, will . . . What if every solar body was an Earth filled with people?

When we declare God as omniscient, we are just speaking words we cannot know. We have no real concept of the meaning of that phrase or of the God who is it. What we do have is relative only to our own finite existence in our world, in our solar system, in our galaxy. But our tiny, little planet is only one of the planets in one solar system. Our solar system is only one of the billions of similar and non-similar solar systems in our galaxy, the Milky Way. In the universe, it has been estimated there are more than 10,000,000,000,000,000,000,000,000,000 galaxies (10 to the 27th power) like the Milky Way. Those are just the galaxies scientists estimate we can see. We have no idea what else God has that we cannot see. This number is just our physical reality and does not count God's spiritual, unseen realities. To say God *is* knowledge is to say God knows all of the knowledge of each of these worlds and realities, and He knows infinitely more than just these realities He created. He also knows every tiny intricacy of every reality He is capable of creating.

Let us also consider that God knows all of this knowledge and He has always known it. It is a part of who, what, when, where, and why He is. God had no beginning, no point in time where learning began. God is knowledge, and **has always been** all knowledge (Isa 40:13-17). God was not taught these things. He did not learn all these things while he was "growing up." God never grew. Growing implies change, and God does not change. He always is, and always will be (Rev. 1:8). There was no beginning to God. We have a beginning. We are finite. He is infinite. God is the only "unbeginning" reality, the only really real . . . whatever He is. His knowledge is a part of who, what, when, where, why He is. If you could add even one jot, or one tittle to his knowledge, He would not have been God until that jot or tittle of knowledge was in Him. He is perfect and complete within Himself, which means He already has all of the jots and tittles of all knowledge, and has always had them. That is what makes Him God. Still, we are not finished.

God **is** all of this knowledge, and He is all knowledge, all at the same time. God does not stop thinking about you so that He can start thinking about me. God knows about you and me and all of everything else we have considered, and He knows it all at the same time. If God could forget or remember or concentrate on a subject, that would be a change. Perfection does not change. Perfection has no need of change. Perfect is already complete. Perfect does not get better. Infinitely complete cannot become more complete.

By now, all of these concepts are only words on a page. Your mind has quit processing and imagining and is just filing away these facts because the fallen, finite mind of man cannot go to where infinite God is. Because we cannot go there or even imagine the infinite majesty of God, we live with an understanding of God, that in our reality, exists or is concocted of what we can comprehend of God from what He has shown of Himself to men that live in a broken state of awareness. This limited understanding is not God to His fullest. It is our concept of God, based on what we as humans can experience, imagine, and conceive. The God of our limited understanding is a conceptual God. Men

Understanding the Bible as History

create profiles of God, assimilating them from those facts about Himself that He has revealed to us, facts that we are able to comprehend. Because we do not all study the written record completely (The Bible) and because we rely upon others to interpret it for us, no two humans "see" God in the same way. Some call Him a Father because they can know what that means. Some who grew up without a father see God as a mother image. (This is not incorrect. God is all things, and God is a mother. His name, El Shaddai, is best translated as Breasted One or Nursing Mother). We say He has an arm or a voice or breath because those things are relative items God has employed in Biblical scriptures to help us understand Him. God is every one of those things and so much more. In order to get His message to us, He has manifested Himself in ways that are purposely relative to our understanding as men.

God is an unimaginable concept. When man records words about God in a book, they are limited by what man can conceive and what he can know of God as a limited, finite being. Man is limited in how he can explain what he knows and is limited by what others can understand of what he knows and is able to explain. Man's words, inspired or not, may or may not reflect the truest reality of God. Those words may or may not reflect the absolute intentions of God for man. That is not to say the Bible is incorrect or should not be used for the purposes of knowing God (2 Tim 3:16). It does suggest the Bible may fall short of saying all there is to say; it is to say, contradiction in the Bible can be caused by man's inability to understand, conceive, or relate concepts between realities. I suggest God designed that contradictions can be sorted out only by reviewing the whole of the Bible in light of itself, using His Holy Spirit to aid in the deciphering, a process that takes time and effort. I suggest this is the reason *Straight is the gate, and narrow is the way, which leadeth unto life, and few there be that find it.* (Matt 7:14).

The Bible tells us that God is all powerful (2Chron 20:6), and all knowing (1Sam 2:3), and able to provide our way (2Cor. 9:8). The Bible also tells us God loves us (John 3:16), is calling us to Himself, and has been guiding each of us to Himself throughout time (2 Tim 1:9). Because of these attributes and provisions of God, we can be confident that what we need to know about God and His Kingdom will be provided to us. If we consider the history of how our Bible came to be, and do so in the light of these same attributes and provisions of God, we should be just as confident that our Bible is one of God's tools to bring us on our way. We can trust that the words in our Holy scriptures are in place to guide us as near to that truest, absolute reality of God that we finite human beings can be led (2Tim. 3:16-17). As the scriptures point out time and time again, especially in the Old Testament (for instance, the book of

Daniel), when words of God recorded by man have gone as far as possible to bring a person on his way to knowing God and God requires more still, He shows up in one form or another. I suggest God is the anonymous Author behind the words, "When the pupil is ready, the Teacher will come."

God always has a way to speak to men. For example, God might instruct someone, "Tell them there is one law, and two rules. **I'll take it from there.**" Although God spoke to one person, and you might see something in that person's words, the "I'll take it from there," suggests something exceptionally beyond, and is meant to address future events that are specifically between you and God. Speaking with God, hearing from God, and visitations upon men by messengers of God in both the Old and New Testaments were common, everyday events before the Dark Ages of world history.

ELIMINATING CONTRADICTION

The cryptic record may cause some Bible contradictions, but these may be eliminated by any who seek the answer from God with ears that are willing to hear. Rendering powerless the contradictions caused by humanism, Bible diving, and ignorance of the scriptures (the foremost causes of Bible contradiction) is a matter of knowing the Bible record. The dichotomy of the Bible is another matter. Dichotomy is written into the record and often times reads confusingly because it is recorded from man's point of view. For instance, Genesis and Exodus display a God who says He will set aside people to Himself and He will care for them and nurture them. God sets up a series of rules which, over a short course of time, the people disobey repeatedly. Then Moses records a conversation with God. In that conversation, God tells Moses He was sorry that He ever made man, and now He will destroy these people. Moses argues with God about it, and God changes His mind (Ex32:11-14, also Gen6:6-7). This program alludes to an immature God that changes. Such displays in Bible narratives have been perceived by those outside the wisdom and knowledge of God, as a God in embryo who is learning, and changing as He goes. Only a thorough study of the whole Bible will show that God is above anger, change, and repentance, and that something other than the events disclosed in this narrative was going on between the recorded lines (Numbers 23:19, I Sam 15:29). This is contradiction caused by the dichotomy of two opposing records—the way God really is, and the way man interpreted Him to be.

Finite humans have a shallow comprehension of infinite God. Having been separated from true Spiritual reality, man's interpretations of God are relative to what he can see and what he is able to comprehend, using his fallen wisdom, knowledge, and experiences. Likewise, finite humans have a shallow comprehension of infinite God's recorded words. In order to comprehend God's Truth, to understand God's words in the Bible as they were designed, a relationship with God is required. Only by a dialogue with the Author of the Bible can we interpret each verse as it was intended. Let me put this idea into perspective.

GONE WITH THE WIND

In considering what is truth, we must contemplate how one can know truth is true, especially in our interpretation of written words. Do we always understand the author's meaning behind the words? Or are those words interpreted differently by each individual reading them? To examine this issue, let us take as an example the great American novel, *Gone With the Wind*.

If we are in search of understanding the truths behind the words of this classic, our best method would be to talk to Margaret Mitchell, the author. She has long since departed from this world, so this may prove impossible. Failing that, the studious might be content to read and reread the book, trying to piece together an understanding. These students may memorize the pages so that anyone could ask, "What is written on line four, paragraph two, page two-hundred twenty-one?" and the student could quote the line forward or backward. The student might be able to give biographical sketches of each character, establishing a life for each that seems to bring these characters off the printed page and into life. But until these students know the author, they really have nothing more than a good guess and a critic's opinion.

Did Margaret Mitchell's parents have a butler named Rhett who was a real man's man, devoted to those he loved, yet secretly a "bad boy?" What happened between her and her parents that made her create the character of Scarlet so independent, defiant, and calculating, yet sometimes confused and frail? Any actual truth beyond what can be superficially imagined from the writing on the pages, can come only from a conference with the author.

Truth can be varied. There is the *opinion truth* that is assumed from superficial knowledge, and there is the *real truth* as was intended by the only one who could know for sure, the author or source. In this light, the Bible is no different from any other book. Unless we know the Author personally, truths as they are interpreted by the various students who study them may also be varied. To find any truth God would have us to know about His scriptures, it is best to talk to Him. He is the Author (2 Tim 3;16, 2 Pet. 1:21). Only then can we know the real design behind the words He has intended. This idea may sound foreign to some, but God has made our task of understanding the scriptures and our purpose in this life here on Earth much easier by allowing us to know Him. God's Anointing, the Holy Spirit, our Teacher, serves as a channel of communication between God and man, bringing the scriptures and the lessons of life to our understanding.

NOTES

1. "Kosmos" is a Greek word translated as "world" and is analogous to our English word "cosmos" defined as "the universe conceived as an orderly and harmonious system." I chose the Greek spelling in order to call attention to the Biblical inference to the Kosmos as a "world order" or " world system." The Biblical Kosmos is a system or order and is the result of evil or selfish decisions fouling the plans of God for man, turning them from their God-designed path. An illustration might be useful here: John So-and-so began the So-and-so Institute of Music in 1798. He died in 1856 leaving the institute in the hands of a board of directors. The institute still teaches music today by the power of those who followed the founder, and this institute teaches according to founder John So-and-so's guidelines even though John So-and-so has been dead for one hundred and fifty years.

The Kosmos is the world system that has been growing ever since the fall of man. It is a system founded on the united principles of many personal realities that have been compromised by evil or by selfish decisions. The Kosmos, or world system, has been founded, set into motion, and like the So-and-so Institute of Music, continues on even after the founders of this errant reality have gone. The Kosmos continues to train those associated with it into the ways of the world system, and those associated with it continue to update and propagate the Kosmos reality.

2. A dichotomy is a differentiation into two contrasted or sharply opposing groups.

Chapter 5

The Teacher

Many may argue that God does not talk to people. Mockers make fun of those who claim God speaks to them. Most who make light of such experiences do not realize how God does speak, and so they appreciate His intercourse with them as only their own conscience, or intuition, or common sense (Rom. 2:14-15). Nevertheless, it is that consciousness of God in us that warns us not to go down that dark alley or to beware of certain persons. God in us is the reason we know our child is in trouble even though that trouble is invisible to our eyes. Most everyone has been privy to an intuitive experience and is aware of events similar to those of which I speak. These events surface most often as an uncommon awareness to something not quite right. Call it what you will—human reasoning, intuition, street smarts—but God's knowledge and wisdom spoken to us through the Teacher in us presents us with ideas, impressions, suggestions, and recommendations we would have no other way of knowing except it was revealed to us by something outside of ourselves.

Intuitive events that protect us and our loved ones are the result of God's Spirit speaking insight into our spirits; though we often claim them as our own, so are many of the fresh ideas, inventions, and solutions to problems that come in our sleep, meditations, and daydreams. God has ensconced the Spirit, or Teacher, in each of us as both a safety measure of protection and as a blessed guide. The Teacher is present by Godly design and intent and is part of God's commitment to our good through His covenant with mankind. Few of us realize our own good conscience is the Teacher or voice of God, put within us to teach, to guide, and to shield us (Job 33:14-18).

Once we learn there are two voices to our conscience—the voice of our own selfish human nature and the voice of the Teacher—then we can begin to separate the two and know one from the other. The voice of God is unselfish, caring, and always interested in what is good for all of creation. Our own selfish human nature is just the opposite, thinking always of self. That voice inside of us is self-centered. One of these two voices or consciences rules us at all times. Those who know God and know the Bible can recognize the Teacher readily; they have come into fellowship with Him and know the benefits of following His lead (How? Acts 2:38; Who? Acts: 10:45 gentiles are all the people of the world; What? Hebrews 6:4-5). Those who fail to recognize His presence, have not come into fellowship with God, nor do they speak God's language. Not-God humanists make themselves known by their words and deeds (Matt. 7:15-20).

For the purpose of teaching, I have named God's language, *Bible*. Bible is a language just like Italian or English is a language. Anyone who can speak a second language fluently will tell us fluency comes when the speaker begins to think the language as opposed to merely trying to piece words together to make a sentence. It is thus with the language of Bible as well. By knowing the Bible thoroughly, we become fluent in the language God has manifested to confer with man, and we can know about God, how He acts, what He does, and why He does what He does. Then, when God does something or when our conscious thoughts are impressed to do other than planned (often this is God speaking to us), we see Him at work and/or hear His advice. If we do not speak the language or are unfamiliar with His ways, we may not recognize Him or see Him when He acts on our behalf. We might not appreciate His Gift at work for us as other than our own conscience (Acts 2:38; 10:45).

God's Gift to us is called the Anointing, the Holy Spirit, or the Teacher. We are first informed of the Teacher in Isaiah 30: 20-21. We are told there would come a day when our Teacher will no longer be hidden from us, but we would be able to know our Teacher. Whenever we have decisions to make we will hear an informative (conscience) voice telling us, "This is the way you should go."

Jesus also told us of the Teacher in John 14:26: *But the Comforter, which is the **Holy Ghost**, whom the Father will send in my name, he shall **teach** you all things, and bring all things to your remembrance, whatsoever I have said unto you.* This is the language. In 1 John 2:27 we read: *But the **anointing** which ye have received of Him abideth in you, and ye need not that any man **teach** you: but as the same **anointing teacheth** you of all things, and is truth, and is no lie, even as it hath **taught** you, ye shall abide in Him.*

The Teacher was the only means by which the first century church could develop, as there was no handy Bible from which to study. The rudiments of the Bible we have come to know and trust today had its origins in the first century A.D., but compilation was not to begin until well into the second century A.D. The Old Testament Scriptures that were available in the first century were locked away in the temples of the Jewish worship or in Essene libraries and were not readily accessible to the followers of Jesus for study. The only available means by which the first century believers could learn or develop was by personally knowing God, an achievement accomplished by knowing the Teacher—God in them. God's teaching Spirit inside believers was, and still is, the primary source of truth.

The Teacher in us is also the Author of the Bible, the One who knows the meanings behind the words. So, when we have questions about the Bible, we can consult Him to ask and receive His answers (James1:5). I suggest that any proper interpretation or understanding of the Bible depends on the interpreter knowing the ways and will, or better yet, the mind of God concerning those scriptures or interpretations in question. I suggest that one way to know God is to know the Bible thoroughly.

Conflicting Christian doctrines can and probably most often do result from people in leadership capacities failing to hear or listen to the Teacher, God's Anointing. Instead, these leaders mingle God's true intention for a scripture with their own human logic. Though well intentioned, these men and women are often lacking in Bible knowledge. Not knowing how to study or how to receive knowledge from God, they rely on the commentary or seminary teachings of others and add their own logic to reason an answer for themselves. Failing in their duty to study for themselves as required (2 Tim. 2:15) and to seek their answers from God, they entrust their office to others. By neglecting to seek God's interpretation for themselves, they create confusion.

God is not a liar (Num. 23:19), nor is He the author of confusion (1Cor. 14:33). His Holy Spirit is here to teach us everything we need to know (1John 2:27). We do not need commentaries or seminaries to understand the Words of God. He has designed that we can come straight to Him. This is not to say that we cannot or should not read a book such as this or listen to lessons from the pulpit. It is to say that we should put such books or lessons on trial and prove them by the Spirit or Teacher in us and by the words that God gave us through the Bible.

Allow me to put all of this into perspective. Right now, in this room where I am writing, there is no television or radio. Should I therefore assume there is no such thing as television or radio? Of course not. In fact, this tiny room is filled with all kinds of radio waves. There are hundreds of television and public radio stations beaming short wave and long wave radio beams through this room as I type. That does not take into account all of the Ham radio, C.B., Walkie Talkie, cell phone, and micro waves that are also present. If radio waves had color, my bet is the visibility in this room would be zero. So why can I not see or hear what is going on in the world outside of this room?

In order to hear what is being said on these radio waves, I would need a receiver with an antenna, a tuner, and speakers somewhere in this room. The receiver will interpret and download to the speakers any message carried on the radio waves. The radio waves will be picked up by the antenna and sorted through by the tuner which identifies each channel of radio waves as they come from the various stations transmitting them.

Now, if I have a receiver but no antenna, I might not hear anything through my speakers. If I have a receiver and an antenna, but my tuner is set between two stations, I might hear static, or I might hear a broken conversation where only every other word is intelligible, or I might hear nothing at all. All of my equipment must be intact and in tune for me to enjoy perfect reception.

Right now, beaming into this room along with all of those radio waves is one Voice that is directed only to me. It is the voice of God speaking personally to my spirit. Now, I might not be able to see God, but does that mean He does not exist? Of course not.

God is telling me something I need for today, something necessary to my purpose that will help to complete His design for my life. He might be saying, "Michael, I want you to go down to Riverside Drive, to the hospital there by the river, room 1230, and say to the man on his death bed: "By the way George, God has need of you to be a fisher of men. Get up and come with me, and God will heal you." (Compare Acts 9:10-16; Acts chap. 10)

Now, if my "God-receiver" is broken or has yet to be installed (through my lack of commitment to the Lord), I might miss this message altogether. If my receiver is intact, but my antenna is not up (caused by my lack of Bible knowledge or my inability to speak Bible), once again, I might not catch the message. If my receiver is installed and my antenna is up, but my tuner is set toward my "business channel" or my "sports channel" instead of toward God, I might only catch every other word. The message I might hear God say is, "Michael, go down to the river at 12:30, by George, and fish!" From this analogy you might see why there is disagreement among the many religions and denominations serving the Living God who has but one perfect message.

I suggest that to hear God, we **must know** God. We must have a relationship with Him, and we must speak the language of Bible fluently. Accuracy comes by much asking through prayer and personal study (meditate in Psalm 119), and not by studying the studies of others who have come before (2 Tim 2:15). If any of those Bible-studying forefathers were incorrect in their interpretations, then every one who follows their commentary lead will be wrong as well. If you are challenged by scripture and need commentary references, take these commentary notes as suggestions and prove them by the Teacher in you and by scripture. Now, let us launch our own education in Godliness, beginning with the Perfect Law.

Chapter 6

Getting Started

The Perfect Law is referred to in the Holy Bible only once by name and is called **"The Perfect Law of Liberty"**(James 1:25). In the same book, the Epistle of James, it is referred to again but only by the name **"Law of Liberty"**(James 2:12). There can be no doubt, James understood the Perfect Law. If the book of James is read in the light of the entire constitution of the Perfect Law, parts of it are much more compelling. This is true of the Bible as a whole. Without the understanding of the Perfect Law, portions of the Bible might be confusing.

Although the reasons for creating each law and rule in the Bible are not often mentioned, by Biblical example it is plain God introduced the Perfect Law of Liberty to guide man into bridling his free will and, in particular, his liberty to do as he selfishly desires. Control of the reins to that bridle, however, are held **by man, not by God**. Man is free to choose his own way, as *"liberty"* implies. Wherever the reins guide the law, the law will go, the law will do, and the law will work, but **always with consequences to the one who holds the reins**.

The Perfect Law of Liberty in no way impedes our dominion or our free will. On the contrary, this law is emancipating; we are encouraged to use our liberty powers. But be assured, if our liberty is used positively, we benefit, succeed, and progress; if our liberty is used negatively, we reap no benefits and may lose some of the benefits we have. This is the lesson in the story Jesus told about the talents (Matt 25:14-30). There are consequences for both obedience and disobedience to every law, and the Perfect Law is no exception. Contrary to popular belief, not all of the rich get richer, and not all of the poor get poorer. It is the Perfect Law that dictates the outcome.

A positive aspect of the Perfect Law of Liberty is this: knowing the constitution of the Law and understanding the consequences that can arise from ignoring or disobeying the Law guides our common sense toward good and Godliness and away from any negative. **A *follower* of**

the Law will eventually be led to acknowledge the Creator of the Law. Because of this one property, I am arguably adamant that understanding and employing the Perfect Law is enough to get us where we need to be in order to find enlightenment as God has prepared it in the Christ. Salvation is our experience, but it is God's accomplishment in us. We need only be attentive and then receptive.

A negative aspect of this Law is that it is self-correcting through punishment. The Law, when transgressed, finds a way to bring the wrong back to center, punishing the transgressor in the process. Use of the Law incorrectly will keep a transgressor spiraling downward until he gets so low he turns to the Creator for help. This is the object lesson of the story Jesus told of "The Prodigal Son." (Luke 15: 11-32) What a wonderful, purpose-filled, God-designed Law! Both obedience and disobedience to the Perfect Law will lead us to find the Creator.

To further explain the Perfect Law, it might be helpful to reexamine and better define some of the Biblical words we use in our everyday language. Some of these words have become maligned to embody adverse connotations. By our reexamination we can diffuse some of these words that have been emotionally loaded with preconceived ideas, thus eliminating any misunderstanding that might hinder or derail the learning process.

SIN

The word *sin* is one of those emotionally loaded, sometimes misused, and often abused words that has caused problems between the secular world and the religious world throughout the ages. The word *sin* has been used by religionists to separate the good from the bad, righteousness from evil, dark from light . . . well, one can only imagine the problems that could arise by its use. This word *sin*, because it has been so misused, has probably caused more arguments than any other word in history.

Sin is actually a benign word. It is purported to be a sporting term common to either 17th century England or the Greek/Roman eras although the etymology of the word bears reference to neither. Still, tradition purports that King James' English translators used the sporting term idea when translating the Greek word for *sin, hamartano, as* a word referring to an error or of missing the mark. According to traditional tales, King James' translators saw in the translation, a likeness to an archer's arrow missing the bull's eye of a target and the purported sporting term for an arrow missing its mark was known as a *sin*. Though there seems little evidence to support the archer/arrow story, and we have no real indication of the origin of this definition, a *sin* is

Getting Started

still translated by most Bible experts today, as an error or the missing of a mark intended.

In the twenty-first century, the idea of missing the mark has been mostly displaced by religionists and a negative value has been ascribed to the word *sin*, instead. Today, this word has become emotionally overloaded with misdirected ideas. When *sin* is used in a religious context, it may easily be mistaken as an insult to imply someone has missed the truth, God, or the righteous way. Throughout history, religionists have expressed the word *sin* in ways intended to **cause** a man to feel he has failed to find the mark, and thus **cause** him to seek repentance. Such expression may call some, but it may also discourage others from wanting to embrace the Bible or a religion as a worthy instrument to bring men to knowledge of God.

An experienced man or woman of the Judeo-Christian faith knows it is God who changes a man's heart (Ezek. 11:19; 36:26), and it is God who both calls men to Himself (1Tim. 1:9; Gal 1:6) and receives them when they come (Psalm 51:10 leads to Ezekiel 36:25-28). Anyone could well use the word *cow* or *tree* to interest a man in knowing God if it is God who is authoring and finishing a person's faith (Hebrews 12:2). If the word *sin* is used improperly, the expression may imply more than a missing of a mark or a fall just short of God's intentions for us. A cursory reading of the Bible will show that although sinning is considered an err against God, a sin, even in religious terms, will not keep one from finding and knowing God.

Selfishness, and sin due to selfishness are a part of the nature of a human being (Romans 3:23). It is our inheritance from the first man Adam (Romans 5:23). The consciousness of God (God calling us), when contrasted against our selfish sinful nature, leads to repentance, which brings us to God. In a round-about way, we might consider sin as a necessary part of spiritual growth, much like a link in a chain is necessary to complete the chain or a rung on a ladder is necessary to the whole of the ladder. We certainly do not want to promote any idea that sinning will lead us to God because selfish men will twist this idea and use it as an excuse to sin. Rather, the point to be made is a solitary sin may not necessarily be a harmful thing or keep us from finding and knowing God. A sin is merely the missing of a mark intended to be hit.

Consider a toddler learning to walk. Mom holds him up while Dad calls from a few steps away. The child takes that first step only to lose his balance and fall down. The child missed the mark intended by the parents, which was to walk from point A to point B. No real consequences, no harm was done. The child just *sinned*. You as the parent would not be angry or apply punishment. One might even say that the child's *sin* was a necessary pathway to finding his balance and learning how to walk.

Now let us say that child decides on his own to take a step, this time unaided by Mom or Dad. He pulls himself up by a chair, turns, and takes one step forward, only to fall again. Again there were no real consequences as no harm was done. Twice the child *sinned* and still the parents were not angry, nor did they apply punishment. In fact, the parents may be encouraged by the child's purely selfish attempt, and might reward the child for attempting to walk on his own. (Sometimes the human nature of selfishness has its place for positive good.)

Now, that same child is crawling toward the edge of that cliff with the 1500 foot drop off. The parent turns to see the child pull himself to a standing position by way of that sign that reads, *"Do not walk beyond this point."* What ensues from the parent to the child is the true meaning behind the scripture verse, *For whom the Lord loveth he correcteth; even as a father the son in whom he delighteth.* (Prov. 3:12, 13:24, Heb 12:6-11) The Bible teaches that if we are not chastised by the Lord when we do wrong, we are not His child, suggesting there is no love between the two. We can fill in the rest of the blanks, but by these examples, we can see that *sin* is merely the missing of a mark. We can also see that sinning can be a part of growing, learning, and achieving. Lastly, we can see that missing the mark can be harmless or have the most dire consequences.

INIQUITY

Iniquity is the step beyond the sin. An iniquity is a series of like sins that are purposely committed. When a person misses the mark on purpose, by choice, time and time again, so much so that he begins making excuses for the sin while using it as a means to fulfill his own selfish, un-God-like desires, he has crossed over into the commission of an iniquity. The thief who will not work to find a job but would rather steal to feed his family and does so with the excuse, "If I don't steal, my kids don't eat," has most likely fallen to an iniquity. Iniquity knows no bounds. It can be as grotesque as the fallen imagination of man can take it. However, it must be said, iniquities are dealt with by God in the same loving manner as with the simplest missing of a mark. Seeking forgiveness with a truly repentant heart is the only requirement to receive full forgiveness from God for a sin or iniquity.

TRANSGRESSION

A *transgression* occurs when someone disregards a rule of God. For example, the Ten Commandments, or rules for good moral character, were put in place by God to serve as signposts at the edge of our cliffs. To disobey these rules would constitute a transgression. Disobeying a rule of God does not affect God; it affects only the life of the transgressor as he meets with the consequence on the other side. The transgression is a sin against a rule of God, but the after-effect is against the transgressor himself.

TRESPASS

A *trespass* is like a transgression, however the trespass is committed against another person or persons and not against God directly. I would suggest we take into account the teaching of Jesus who said in Matthew 25:31-46, *inasmuch as ye have done it unto one of the least of these my brethren, ye have done it unto me.* Considering this, a trespass against another individual is also a trespass against the Son of God, and indirectly a transgression against the rule of God to love one another as He loves us (John 13:34-35). The words "trespass" and "transgression" are used interchangeably throughout the Bible; I suggest this is so to reflect this idea. Not to help a neighbor in trouble is a trespass but might also be considered a transgression.

DEED

A deed is the finished work of an act or action. A deed is what our actions or our works produce and can be tangible or intangible. There are positive deeds and negative deeds.

All of our works or actions produce deeds. Our works are measured by the deeds they accomplish. A good deed is proof that a positive work has been accomplished. A positive work is a righteous, moral, unselfish action. The positive deed is the proof of a work of Godliness and faith (James 2:14-26).

A negative deed is just the opposite. A negative deed is proof that a negative work has been accomplished. A negative work is an act of selfishness (Not-God). The negative deed is the finished work of a sin, iniquity, trespass, transgression, or a combination of any or all of these. When a deed is negative, the *deed* joins the list of the other "components of corruption," sin, iniquity, trespass, and transgression. The negative deed is the fifth component of corruption.

The importance of the *deed* is little recognized, yet the "good deed" is the substantial cause of most all of our blessings. As a negative component of corruption, the "bad deed" is the substantial cause of most all of the problems in our world today. Our total ignorance of the importance of the deed is the major cause of mankind's undoing, individually and corporately. Without knowledge of the deed, man cannot answer the question *"why?"*. If man does not understand what is causing his problems, he will not be able to fix them. For this reason, we need to rediscover the power and the potential of the deed.

The negative deed is the finished work or end result of a transgression, trespass, iniquity, or sin. It can be tangible or intangible. Consider these explications:

The negative tangible deed: A person gets into an altercation with another individual and in the heat of the argument, pulls a gun, shoots his opponent, and kills him. The perpetrator has committed a sin with dire consequences by missing the mark of how he should have morally and righteously handled the altercation. He has committed a transgression against the rule, *Thou shall not kill*. He has also committed numerous trespasses against another human being, the victim's family, his friends, and his children born and yet unborn. Finally, he has created a deed, the finished work of a sin, iniquity, transgression, or trespass. The man lying before him is now lifeless.

The perpetrator may immediately realize his sin and ask forgiveness of God for both his sin and his transgression against God's rule. If he does so with a truly repentant heart, he will be forgiven. If he then goes to the family and admits his wrong doing, and with the same heart asks forgiveness of the family, friends, and children of the deceased, he may get their forgiveness as well. By his repentance, the sin, transgression, and trespass have been dealt with. However, the tangible deed lives on because the victim is still dead. The corpse is real.

The negative intangible deed: Whether the perpetrator pulls a gun or merely shoots the "bullet" of insult ("You're so stupid!" "You're so ugly!" "Nobody likes you!"), the damage is done. Like the tangible deed, the damage created by an intangible deed lives on. Once created, the intangible deed of gossip or insult remains stored in the victim's computer-like brain and for a lifetime has an effect on every future thought and decision made.

Deeds cannot be undone. A shattered glass bottle can be reconstructed with glue or melted down and remade, but it is never the exact same bottle again. Sins, iniquities, trespasses, and transgressions are spiritual and may be undone (forgiven). A negative deed is the finished work of corruption. It becomes a living entity and enters our physical reality. No one can undo a deed. At best, it can be compensated.

I suggest this inability to undo a deed is the reason God instituted the Perfect Law. Because a deed created becomes a permanent fixture in our reality, God wants to make us acutely aware that there are consequences to every deed. There is no better way to accomplish this than to make each of us personally responsible for the deeds we create. God designed that the deeds we turn loose to do damage or good come back to us in the same manner to affect us personally. By the Perfect Law, God made sure we would realize what we are doing. We will be rewarded justly for what we personally produce in the world, receiving good for the good we do and bad for the bad we do. Whatever we do will be returned upon us as though we are doing it to or for ourselves.

God was merciful to design into the Perfect Law ways to reverse **the consequences** of a negative deed. Any negative deed can be turned around when the doer of the selfish deed recognizes his or her foolishness, seeks forgiveness, and makes compensation for the deed. But know this—**every deed *will* be justly recompensed**—if not by our own choice and actions, then by the Perfect Law.

What a Perfect Law! God had a perfect design to make life fair for everyone by encouraging us to create positive deeds that would return good to us, and avoid negative deeds that would return to hurt us. God knows, even our natural, selfish human nature would drive us to respond to such a law positively once we know and understand how the Law affects us personally. How perfect is that?

It is important to note that even with forgiveness granted and compensation made, the deed itself lives on. The finished work (deed) of a sin, iniquity, trespass, or transgression can never be totally undone. It is a living entity that continues to do damage. I suggest this is the reason overcompensation is required. I also suggest it is the reason we should become acutely aware of our every decision to bring forth a deed.

If we gossip, gossip will come back upon us. However, even when we stop gossiping, the gossip we already put forth is still out there working and doing damage. Making compensation may involve confessing our sins one to another (1John 1:9), thus undoing the lie told in the gossip to stop it from doing more harm.

If we bring a law suit against another to extract money in excess of our loss, we will lose more (Exodus 21:24-25; Leviticus 24:20-22). The Bible says we are to make peace with our brothers before we get to court (Matt 5:25-26; Luke 12:58-59). If we stole, we must never again steal, but rather make compensation by working with our hands to give to those who are poor and in dire need. This will help them and lessen their need to survive by unethical means (Eph. 4:28). Deed compensation is written throughout the Bible, but often it is not named for what it is. Like a buried treasure yet to be uncovered, the Perfect Law's attributes, consequences, and compensations can be made known to us only if we seek them out.

In our quest to understand the intricacies of the deed, the question arises: what provisions has God designed concerning the deed? In human terms—what does God "think" about the deed? It is not so important what we think about the deed from our humanistic logic and reasoning, nor is it important how we think we should deal with the deed according to our broken philosophical *isms*. It is important to know what is God's design concerning the deed.

It is the deed, tangible and intangible, that is the subject of the Perfect Law. Much to man's chagrin, it is the negative deed, tangible and intangible, that is his downfall. The Perfect Law was put in motion **specifically to govern the deed**. To understand how God deals with the deed we must first know what God says about deeds, and then we must ascertain how God has dealt with them throughout mankind's history, thus the necessity for a journal (the Bible) recording the histories of man back to the beginning of time.

Chapter 7

Making it Real

Before we get into the constitution of the Perfect Law, let me share the pathway that led me to discover and then decipher this Law. Part of my understanding the Perfect Law involved God making it relative to my reality. I suggest that in order to know and employ the Perfect Law, each of us must be aware of it in our own experience, how it works, what it has accomplished, and what it can do. Here is how my eyes were opened.

I was sitting alone in my home office in October of 1981 with the television playing quietly in the corner when a breaking news story interrupted the programming. Anwar Sadat, the President of Egypt, had been assassinated in an attempted military coup designed to take over the Egyptian government. The coup failed, but the deed was done. Anwar Sadat's corpse was real. Hosni Mubarak, President Sadat's then Vice-President, took office and still serves today as the President of Egypt.

I paid attention because at that time, the Christian church was embroiled in debates about the end times and how the culmination of those end times would find itself in the Middle-East. Having studied the arguments, I was somewhat familiar with the daily events of the Middle East. My first thought after the news broke was not about the end of the world, but rather was a question to God. Why Sadat? This man seemed like such a man of peace and a bridge between the vacillating powers in the region. If anyone could have made a difference, I imagined it would be Anwar Sadat. He was an Arab Muslim peace maker, (I found later he was married to a European, Christian wife), working with Israel toward peace with other Arab nations.

The news stayed on the event most of the day, and during the course of the media exposé it came out that Anwar Sadat had advanced in the Egyptian government in the same manner in which he was killed. Sadat had participated in the military-led coup of 1952 to dethrone the then reigning King of Egypt, Farouk I. The coup was successful, and afterwards Sadat staked his claim in the Egyptian government. As a result, he later became President. I remember thinking what a coincidence that was. His career began with a coup, and it ended with a coup.

That evening in my Bible studies, a scripture jumped off the page at me. It was Galatians 6:7 *Be not deceived; God is not mocked: for whatsoever a man soweth, that shall he also reap.* I made serious note of that scripture, knowing that somehow it related to the events I had witnessed earlier in my day. Although I did not know it at the time, God had answered my question of why through a single Bible verse. Without even realizing it, this verse set me on a new pathway of discovery. I was about to uncover the Perfect Law.

Sometime later, I was preparing for a Bible study on the life of King David. In the course of my research, the scriptures below were opened to me in a way I had never seen them before. These scriptures document a small portion of the life of King David. In them are some noticeable parallels between the rules David had disobeyed and the punishments he received as a result. The parallels seemed to reflect the coincidences I had seen a few weeks earlier through the death of Anwar Sadat. The idea is that the things we do have a commonality with the things that are done to us.

2 Samuel 11

¹And it came to pass, after the year was expired, at the time when kings go forth to battle, that David sent Joab, and his servants with him, and all Israel; and they destroyed the children of Ammon, and besieged Rabbah. But David tarried still at Jerusalem. ²And it came to pass in an evening-tide, that David arose from off his bed, and walked upon the roof of the king's house: and from the roof he saw a woman washing herself; and the woman was very beautiful to look upon. ³And David sent and inquired after the woman. And one said, Is not this Bathsheba the daughter of Eliam, the wife of Uriah the Hittite? ⁴And David sent messengers and took her: and she came in unto him, and he lay with her; (for she was purified from her uncleanness:) and she returned unto her house. ⁵And the woman conceived, and sent and told David, and said, I am with child. ⁶And David sent to Joab, saying, Send me Uriah the Hittite. And Joab sent Uriah to David. ⁷And when Uriah was come unto him, David demanded of him how Joab did, and how the people did, and how the war prospered. ⁸And David said to Uriah, Go down to thy house, and wash thy feet. And Uriah departed out of the king's house, and there followed him a mess of meat from the king.

⁹But Uriah slept at the door of the king's house with all the servants of his lord, and went not down to his house. ¹⁰And when they had told David, saying, Uriah went not down unto his house, David said unto Uriah, Camest thou not from thy journey? why then didst thou not go down unto thine house? ¹¹And Uriah said unto David, The ark, and Israel, and Judah, abide in tents; and my lord Joab, and the servants of my lord are encamped in the open fields; shall I then go into mine house, to eat and to drink, and to lie with my wife? as thou livest, and as thy soul liveth, I will not do this thing. ¹²And David said to Uriah, Tarry here to-day also, and to-morrow I will let thee depart. So Uriah abode in Jerusalem that day and the morrow. ¹³And when David had called him, he did eat and drink before him; and he made him drunk: and at even he went out to lie on his bed with the servants of his lord, but went not down to his house. ¹⁴And it came to pass in the morning, that David wrote a letter to Joab, and sent it by the hand of Uriah. ¹⁵And he wrote in the letter, saying, Set ye Uriah in the forefront of the hottest battle, and retire ye from him, that he may be smitten, and die. ¹⁶And it came to pass, when Joab observed the city, that he assigned Uriah unto a place where he knew that valiant men were. ¹⁷And the men of the city went out, and fought with Joab: and there fell some of the people of the servants of David; and Uriah the Hittite died also. ¹⁸Then Joab sent and told David all the things concerning the war; ¹⁹And charged the messenger, saying, When thou hast made an end of telling the matters of the war unto the king, ²⁰And if so be that the king's wrath arise, and he say unto thee, Wherefore approached ye so nigh unto the city when ye did fight? knew ye not that they would shoot from the wall? ²¹Who smote Abimelech the son of Jerubbesheth? did not a woman cast a piece of a mill-stone upon him from the wall, that he died in Thebez? why went ye nigh the wall? then say thou, Thy servant Uriah the Hittite is dead also. ²²So the messenger went, and came and showed David all that Joab had sent him for. ²³And the messenger said unto David, Surely the men prevailed against us, and came out unto us into the field, and we were upon them even unto the entering of the gate. ²⁴And the shooters shot from off the wall upon thy servants : and some of the king's servants be dead, and thy servant Uriah the Hittite is dead also. ²⁵Then David said unto the messenger, Thus shalt thou say unto Joab, Let not this thing displease thee, for the sword devours one as well as another: make thy battle more strong against the city, and overthrow it: and encourage thou him. ²⁶And when the wife of Uriah heard that Uriah her husband was dead, she mourned for

her husband. ²⁷And when the mourning was past, David sent and fetched her to his house, and she became his wife, and bare him a son. But the thing that David had done displeased the LORD.

2 Samuel 12

¹2:1 And the LORD sent Nathan unto David. And he came unto him, and said unto him, There were two men in one city; the one rich, and the other poor. ²The rich man had exceeding many flocks and herds: ³But the poor man had nothing save one little ewe lamb, which he had bought and nourished up: and it grew up together with him, and with his children; it did eat of his own meat, and drank of his own cup, and lay in his bosom, and was unto him as a daughter. ⁴And there came a traveler unto the rich man, and he spared to take of his own flock and of his own herd, to dress for the wayfaring man that was come unto him; but took the poor man's lamb, and dressed it for the man that was come to him. ⁵And David's anger was greatly kindled against the man; and he said to Nathan, As the LORD liveth, the man that hath done this thing shall surely die. ⁶And he shall restore the lamb four-fold, because he did this thing, and because he had no pity. ⁷And Nathan said to David, Thou art the man. Thus saith the LORD God of Israel, I anointed thee king over Israel, and I delivered thee out of the hand of Saul; ⁸And I gave thee thy master's house, and thy master's wives into thy bosom, and gave thee the house of Israel and of Judah; and if that had been too little, I would moreover have given unto thee such and such things. ⁹Wherefore hast thou despised the commandment of the LORD, to do evil in his sight? thou hast killed Uriah the Hittite with the sword, and hast taken his wife to be thy wife, and hast slain him with the sword of the children of Ammon. ¹⁰Now therefore the sword shall never depart from thine house; because thou hast despised me, and hast taken the wife of Uriah the Hittite to be thy wife. ¹¹Thus saith the LORD, Behold I will raise up evil against thee out of thine own house, and I will take thy wives before thine eyes, and give them unto thy neighbour, and he shall lie with thy wives in the sight of this sun. ¹²For thou didst it secretly: but I will do this thing before all Israel, and before the sun. ¹³And David said unto Nathan, I have sinned against the LORD. And Nathan said unto David, The LORD also hath put away thy sin; thou shalt not die. ¹⁴Howbeit, because by this deed thou hast given great occasion to the enemies of the LORD to blaspheme, the child also that is born unto thee shall surely die. ¹⁵And

> Nathan departed unto his house. And the LORD struck the child that Uriah's wife bare unto David, and it was very sick. [16]David therefore besought God for the child; and David fasted, and went in, and lay all night upon the earth. [17]And the elders of his house arose, and went to him, to raise him up from the earth: but he would not, neither did he eat bread with them. [18]And it came to pass on the seventh day, that the child died. And the servants of David feared to tell him that the child was dead: for they said, Behold, while the child was yet alive, we spake unto him, and he would not hearken unto our voice: how will he then vex himself, if we tell him that the child is dead? [19]But when David saw that his servants whispered, David perceived that the child was dead: therefore David said unto his servants, Is the child dead? And they said, He is dead. [20]Then David arose from the earth, and washed, and anointed himself, and changed his apparel, and came into the house of the LORD, and worshiped: then he came to his own house; and when he required, they set bread before him, and he did eat. [21]Then said his servants unto him, What thing is this that thou hast done? thou didst fast and weep for the child, while it was alive; but when the child was dead, thou didst rise and eat bread. [22]And he said, While the child was yet alive, I fasted, and wept: for I said, Who can tell whether GOD will be gracious to me, that the child may live? [23]But now he is dead, wherefore should I fast? can I bring him back again? I shall go to him, but he shall not return to me. [24]And David comforted Bath-sheba his wife, and went in unto her, and lay with her: and she bare a son, and he called his name Solomon: and the LORD loved him.

With the discovery of these verses, I found myself on a quest for spiritual enlightenment. The similarity behind the events in President Sadat's life and those in King David's started me thinking there might be a supernatural principle behind what seemed to be coincidental events. In both of their cases, the things they had done were much like the things that were done to them. In David's case, the things that would be done to him were predicted ahead of the events.

I continued my study of King David's life seeking to find if everything Nathan prophesied in 2 Samuel came to pass. My investigation over the next many days proved fruitful. I found the events the prophet predicted not only came to pass, but what happened to David was even worse than what David had done. This was similar to Sudat's fate. By a coup he had dethroned Farouk I, but his fate as a result was worse. Sudat was likewise dethroned and—even worse—killed.

Although I undertook this study with a positive attitude to learn, it had an adverse effect on me. I took serious issue with some of the content of David's story. For instance, in one measure, God told King David through the prophet Nathan that David had transgressed the law. I assumed that meant David had disobeyed the sixth and seventh commandments dealing with murder and adultery. Although David's involvement with Uriah's death was a conspiracy in nature and not a direct consequence of David's hand, Uriah was killed as the result of his orders.

I had come to understand that our current rule of law concerning capital punishment in America is derived from the Bible. The idea for it is drawn in part from Genesis 9:6. The ramifications for David's crime were enormous. King David must die. Yet Nathan sidestepped God's prescribed sentence and imposed a punishment other than death. I took issue with this because I considered that God was overlooking David's crimes. Did God circumvent the law for David? Did God change the prescribed sentence for this crime to benefit a king? At first reading, it sounds as if David is free, and his child would die in his stead. Imagine some of the questions an inquisitive young mind might raise around this incident: God changed His mind? God changed His law? Kings get special treatment?

My consternation piqued when Nathan informed David that because he selfishly killed one man, the sword (a symbol of blood letting and war) would never depart from his house. By this declaration, the warring, killing, deed David himself was guilty of would reside in the family to punish David's children for generations to follow. Wow! Where did that come from? That hardly seemed fair to punish David's family for something he did. I remember feeling troubled over this idea because it did not seem the proper judgement to be given by a forgiving God who loves unconditionally.

I sought out the principles of Biblical law concerning murder, thinking perhaps there was more than just the punishment of death. Maybe there were mitigating circumstances that offered a second punishment. During the course of this study, I encountered the ten commandments, and rediscovered Exodus 20:1-5, wherein it says, . . . *for I the LORD thy God am a jealous God, visiting the iniquity of the fathers upon the children unto the third and fourth generation* . . . I had not comprehended the full scope of this verse when I first discovered it in a study years earlier, but I knew this was the answer. This explained why the sword was allowed upon David's family line. However, the idea put forth in this scripture only added to my conundrum.

So far, my journey had dumped me at the doorstep of confusion. Yes, the similarity between the deed and the return-of-deed appeared to have some spiritual principle guiding it; and yes, the concept that my children might suffer the wrath of God because I had done something stupid in my past was also apparent. Therein lay the major portion of my disturbance. I was unsettled by my love for my children and by the scope of this mandate. However, God knows my thought process, character and personality. He was using these trepidations to drive me deeper into this study. My nature, when I come up against a puzzle, is to enter the labyrinth with zeal and give it my all to find the passage that leads to the golden key. This journey was no different. I entered the race enthusiastically, and in the course of my search discovered the purpose and the power of the Perfect Law.

In archeology, excavating a buried treasure is a painstaking process of finding, digging, burrowing, and removing layer upon layer of earth to reveal the treasure. Though this Law is quite simple to see and define, it took years to quarry because the majority of the times the Law is illuminated in scripture, it is presented subliminally through its attributes and actions and not called by name. For instance, because it is presented so subliminally, it is easy to overlook the Perfect Law as the cause of the flood in Noah's day. It was not God who brought the punishment back to man, but rather the earth itself by the power of the Perfect Law. However, the Bible student might not see this (I had not seen it at first) without an understanding of all of the attributes and the power of the Perfect Law.

One attribute of the Perfect Law, which I suggest is the most important attribute, is **the Perfect Law is the judge, jury, and executor over the laws and rules of God**. God Himself **does not** prosecute the deeds of man. Firstly, the jobs of prosecuting, judging, and executing punishment involve change; secondly, it involves God entering into the events of men uninvited. God has determined He would do neither. God gave man dominion. By Sovereign choice He has determined not to enter into the events of men unless invited. That means God will not judge us or punish us unless we ask Him to judge us and punish us (Where is that line forming?) and Perfect God does not change. Thus, Perfect God created the Perfect Law to prosecute, judge, and execute in His stead.

Another attribute of **the Perfect Law is that it acts without passion and without prejudice**. The Perfect Law is the "gravity" behind each "signpost" in the Bible. When that signpost reads, "do not walk beyond this point," and someone chooses to ignore it, the Perfect Law steps in and delivers the verdict just as faithfully and truly as gravity does when one steps off the cliff—and it does so without partiality to the perpetrator. King or student, male or female, young or old, the Perfect Law is not a respecter of persons. Once again we must go down the road that led to the discovery of these attributes.

The more I explored Biblical law, the more I questioned the very judgement of God. Not that His judgement would be correct or incorrect, fair or unfair, but that God would have any judgement at all. In my mind, the ideology of judgement precluded God's participation. Judgement represents change, and God does not change. (Malachi 3:6) Unlike man, God does not review, reassess, or change his mind. At the time I began this journey, my idea of judging something or someone was to say, "Yesterday I felt one way about this situation, but now that I have seen the evidence and have learned something new, I am reassessing my position." Unwittingly, by applying a humanistic understanding of judgement-by-man to God, I found myself with a philosophical argument that precluded God's involvement in any case of judgement. It would be like saying God did not know the outcome of the situation before it happened, or God did not know all there was to know about a situation as it was happening. Both views express the idea of anti-omniscience. There are no variables with God, no shifting of shadow (James 1:17). God is who He is. God does what He does because He is who He is, and that does not change. When He makes a decree, He does not take back His words. (Isaiah 31:2)

If God could think a new thought, He would not be perfect until that new thought was processed. New ideas represent change. Change represents imperfection. God does not change, nor is there any imperfection in Him. If tomorrow God could be different than He is today, then He could not be God until all of those differences were realized and in place. We do not serve a God in embryo. He is infinitely complete and infinitely perfect. He is self-existent and in need of nothing. There is nothing we can add to God. There is nothing God does not have. There is nothing God does not know. That being said, we have to deal with the contradictions of the Bible that record God judging, repenting, and changing His mind.

Chapter 8
Judgement

All that has been said in these past few pages is leading us to understand God a little better. I pray these explications will help us to better know our Teacher and enrich our understanding of our loving, almighty, Creator God. I pray these will also help us reappraise our limited understanding of God's predilection for mankind, as many are confused about His passion for creation. To the student without fellowship or command of the Bible language, it might seem throughout the chronology of the Bible that God is a punishing, limited god who is learning as he grows, making mistakes but evolving and changing for the better as history carries on. To the learned student who has both a fellowship with the Creator and command of the language of Bible, it is apparent that as man has evolved through the pages of the Bible, his understanding of God has also evolved. The God recorded by man in the Old Testament appears judgmental, egotistical, and vacillating. The God of the New Testament appears as a God of Love, peace, and forgiveness. God did not grow up over the course of history recorded in the Bible; rather, man slowly became a better interpreter of God's true reality through his four thousand years of experience with the Almighty. All of that being said, let us go back to the courtroom and readdress this idea of judgement and God sitting as judge.

If we consider the act of judgement as we visit it in the human courtroom, we will see that judgement is the result of a selective process. Opposing testimonies create differing mind-sets, and the judge and jury are moved back and forth throughout the trial and the selection of the final verdict. It is evident that judgement in the human arena involves change. If judgement involves change, can God, who does not change, enter into the act of judgement? Let me tell you a story.

When my children were little, they would often come to me and tell me they were bored and had nothing to do. I would tell them to go into the back yard and play. I would suggest some parameters of play. For instance, there was a sandbox; I would suggest they take their little people and cars and build a city. They could pretend to be the king of Sandbox City. There was a club house which they could use as a storefront or schoolhouse to play business man or teacher. There was also a swing set. They could jump on the rings and pretend they were the next gold medal contender at the Olympic games. They could use the open space to invent, discover, explore, and do whatever they chose to do. I had only one rule: Do not leave my back yard! I would tell them, "If you do, I will immediately bring you into the house, and you will stand in the corner for half an hour."

Now my children were free to do as they pleased in order to enjoy themselves in the back yard. They were free to invent, discover, explore, and create. If my boys decided to play football and sometime during their game their football went over the fence into the neighbor's yard, would they be free to retrieve it? Let us say the football went over the fence and one of them mindlessly jumped the fence without thinking about the rule I laid down (a rule they were free to misinterpret, abuse, or ignore), grabbed the wayward football, returned to the yard, and without a second thought, returned to play. Would they be guilty of disobeying my rule? Should they be punished?

Now let us say the ball went over the fence, and in the course of climbing the fence, my son saw the rabbit hutch up under the neighbor's window. He looked at the hutch, looked at the window from where I survey my back yard to see if I were watching, looked at the hutch, again at the window, then proceeded over the fence, ignoring the football to head for the rabbit hutch, instead. Now is he guilty of disobeying my rule? Now should he be punished?

My rule "Do not leave my backyard" had a consequence behind it (thirty minutes of corner time). I decreed the punishment at the same moment I decreed the rule. When my son disobeyed my rule, punishment was guaranteed. Would I be wrong to punish him?

From my vantage point at the window, I could see my scope of protection. While my son was in my yard he was in my loving care, and as a watchful parent, I could oversee any event that might bring harm and correct it before any damage was done. My neighbor's yard, on the other hand, was at such an angle only a small portion of the back lot was visible to my watchful eye and my protective abilities. I could not see the rabbit hutch, nor could I see the chained Pit Bull sleeping underneath that hutch.

Had I brought my son inside for disobeying my rule and stood him in the corner as a punishment, would I be guilty of change in any way? Did I change my mind? Did I change my love for my child? The point is, my child disobeyed my rule, and judgement came as a result of his choice to ignore that rule. Any punishment he received, be it cornertime or stitches to his wounds, was a consequence of his own actions according to his own free will and was not a result of some decision I made after the event occurred. My son left the protection of my love and when he did, he entered into judgement. Any aftermath was the result of personal accountability.

I did not change. I did not change my love for my child. I did not change my thoughts about my child. I did not change my thoughts about my rule or the in-the-corner punishment for disobeying my rule. I remained neutral and true to myself and to the rule I made in the beginning to protect my children. The rule itself was my design to protect my children. The rule was their friend—and their judge. **The Perfect Law, acting without passion or prejudice, is our prosecutor, our judge, our jury, and the executor of our punishment and rewards,** not God.

So, can God judge? Does God judge? Can God repent? Does God repent? The answers are yes, yes, yes, and yes, but He does not do these things in the way we finite humans do them. In His infinite wisdom, God created a way to do these things without entering into the doing of them. God created the Perfect Law, and by the power of that Law, judgement and repentance is accomplished in a way that might appear to our finite understanding as God doing what He does not do—change (by judging or repenting). Our God, who does not change, made a sovereign decision. He chose before the creation of this world to oversee and care for it by the power of the Perfect Law. So, in a sense, we might say God is judge because God has chosen a judge—the Perfect Law. God is a judge by proxy. Psalm 37:28 declares, *For the Lord loveth judgment.* Judgement is spoken of here, and in many other places throughout the Bible, as though it is a thing, a separate entity that comes into existence and abides in and of itself. This would be true if God did not actively participate by judging, but allows the Perfect Law to do the judging for Him. Then He would judge (participate in judgement by being the Author, Creator, and the One who sustains the law), yet not be THE judge. As a result, judgement is rendered. God judges, but does not judge, yet renders judgement—just like the Bible says. The sewing needles in our board align concerning this contradiction once we understand how God judges.

As a side-bar, I must address the theologians and philosophers who will read and dissect this appraisal of God's inability to change because making a sovereign choice is a change; I said God made the sovereign choice to create the Perfect Law. Choosing to do something is a change. Yesterday, that change did not exist. Today it does because I chose to implement something different.

If one is to contemplate God, one must philosophically enter the infinite. Imagination is all we have to light that pathway, so do we use my imagination or another's? Because I am the author of this treatise, I will suggest from my own meditations how God might be, and let the Teacher sort it out for those who desire to know Him. In other words, as authority of this work, I will give you my assessment, but we all need to ask God for ourselves.

I suggest that God never implements something different. As there is nothing new under the sun (Eccl. 1:9), there is nothing *different* to implement. I suggest God only implements something *differently*. All options are already in Him. Perfect God **is** all things. Complete God **is** the Perfect Law, like Complete God **is** creation. We might use other words and say that creation is the *way* God is, and the Perfect Law is also the *way* God is. Creation and the Perfect Law are, and have always been, parts of whom, what, when, where, and why God is.

God is Perfect Law. God does not make law, or have law, or do law. He is it, in every way, always! God is all things, and God is Perfect Law. God had no beginning. He has always been and will always be Perfect Law and everything else. What He is, How He is, Who He is, When He is, and Where He is, will always be God the unchangeable.

God is all things, in every way, always. God is creation and God is the Perfect Law. The Perfect Law is not only the way God is, the Perfect Law is the way God does what He does. The Perfect Law is like an organ in the body of God. Creation is like God's skin. Our skin cells do what they do because they are what they are. The cells in our own skin do not perform like brain cells or as stomach cells. They function as skin cells. They do what they do because of what they are.

Our skin cells die and are replaced. Our skin "changes" regularly, but our skin is always skin and is always covering our body parts while we are alive. Our skin is what it is, and it does what it does because it is what it is. Our skin is doing things differently today than yesterday, but our skin is not different from yesterday. We do not have human skin one day and elephant skin the next. That would be different.

Likewise, worlds come and worlds go, but creation always is. Creation and the Perfect Law are not new. They were not something different that God chose to do one day having "thought" them up out of the clear blue sky. Although some words of the Bible are written as though God changes, the words were recorded from, and intended for our finite understanding. The overall picture of God throughout the Bible will allow all of the needles in our board of understanding to align to reveal an unchanging, unchangeable God. Creation and the Perfect Law have always and will always be a part of who, what, when, where, and why God is. *Choice* is a word relative only to the finite.

KING DAVID'S PLIGHT

Let us return to the story of King David. It was here I discovered the existence of the Perfect Law. It was his case that opened my eyes and I saw that something very important, yet mysteriously obscured, had transpired in this narrative. I suggest we read and reread the passages in 2 Samuel 11-12 several times to become familiar with the intricacies of the story before we consider the following.

It was obvious by Nathan's words to Kind David that three deeds had been committed by David and that three punishments would be exacted. The more I meditated in the percussions of these deeds and the repercussions they invoked, the more I noticed the similarity between what was done by David and what was returned upon David. The three deeds mentioned are these: 1 David committed adultery with Bath-sheba, the wife of another man, Uriah the Hittite; 2 David killed Uriah the Hittite, not by his own hands, but by the hands of the children of Ammon; 3 David *despised the commandment of the Lord* (thou shall not kill, thou shall not commit adultery, and I suggest the greatest commandment, Love God above all others, including little god i am) and thereby had given great occasion to the enemies of God to blaspheme. Let us consider these three deeds one at a time.

The first deed is adultery. David committed adultery with Uriah's wife Bath-sheba, and a child was born from their union. Before we can deal fully with this incident, we must come to acknowledge some Biblical/historical facts. These facts were a part of my uncovering this treasure and did not come to me over the weeks ahead, but over the years.

Though David failed in the making of right choices in this narrative, we still have record that God approved of him. David was a man who sought the will of God for his own life (Acts13:22). The scripture says that David's heart was perfect (1Kings 15:3) before God and that he *turned not aside from any thing that He commanded him all the days of His life, save only in the matter of Uriah the Hittite* (1 Kings 15:5). We must take into account that there was more to David's life than the few verses offered in 2 Samuel. We have record of nearly six decades of David and his association to God, to God's covenant, and of David's devotion to the posterity of Israel. Chosen by God, David was an avid student of the scriptures. We can see by his Psalms and his many deeds as warrior and King (recorded in the Old Testament history books of 1 and 2 Samuel, 1 Chronicles, and Psalms), that he knew the books of the law. He understood the covenant of God and the Perfect Law as well or better than any of his peers.

It was unfortunate that David's selfish desires for Bath-sheba preceded God's intentions, but while we are driving the needles of interpretation into the board of understanding, we must agree that according to the Biblical narrative, somewhere in David's future Bath-sheba was an intended wife of David. Otherwise 1Kings 15:5 would read *save only in the matter of Uriah the Hittite,* **and his wife Bath-sheba**. The narrative does not include Bath-sheba as a cause for judgement. The fact that David was punished inordinately for his deed of adultery, but the object of his adultery, Bath-sheba, is not noted in 1Kings 5:5, and the fact that 1Kings 5:5 remembers only the murder of Uriah the Hittite, reveals that Bath-sheba was all along in God's plans for David, but not until Uriah had died of a cause other than murder. The fact that Solomon was God's next choice of Kings (1 Chron. 28:3-10) and that Solomon was born of the union of David and Bath-sheba confirms this (2Sam. 12:24). Regardless, the punishment for adultery had to be administered if God be true to His word.

The punishment for the deed of adultery with Bath-sheba was indeed administered. Nathan warned *Thus saith the Lord, Behold I will raise up evil against thee out of thine own house, and I will take thy wives before thine eyes, and give them unto thy neighbor, and he shall lie with thy wives in the sight of this sun* (2 Sam. 12:11). The punishment for this deed came back upon David in multiples when his own son Absalom raised arms against him (*I will raise up evil against thee out of thine own house)* and chased David from the city. (2Samuel 15). 2 Sam 16:20-22 tells us; *Then said Absalom to Ahithophel, Give counsel among you what we shall do. And Ahithophel said unto Absalom, Go in unto thy father's concubines, which he hath left to keep the house; and all Israel shall hear that thou art abhorred of thy father: then shall the hands of all that are with thee be strong. So they spread Absalom a tent upon the top of the house; and Absalom went in unto his father's concubines in the sight of all Israel.* Nathan had foretold to David that this deed would come back upon him exactly this way. Nathan said someone would commit adultery with David's wives in broad daylight, for all to see.

The second deed is two-pronged. It concerned the killing of another human being, and it concerned the killing of that person by proxy, involving a third party (the children of Ammon (2Sam12:9). The fact that the children of Ammon were noted in scripture and that God thought it important enough Nathan should make mention of the **children of Ammon**, aroused my curiosity. Why mention the descendants of Ammon? Did this act somehow confer the evil deed of David upon an innocent and unsuspecting third party (the children of Ammon). Did it enjoin Ammon's descendants to any punishment as a result of that deed? Reasoning from that premise, I saw the children of Ammon raising arms against a man of God (Uriah). If what they did was somehow to be returned upon them, then it would follow that it would also come back upon the one who caused the deed. I do not believe it is a coincidence that the punishment met to David for this deed was this: 2Sam 12:10 *Now therefore the sword shall **never** depart from **thine house;*** This meant that the sword would always be upon those who were born into the house of David. David caused **the children of Ammon** to be punished. Now David's children would reap what he sowed for the children of another.[1]

It was not long afterwards that this group of David's evil deeds began to return upon him. Although it might have seemed the deeds had gone away, the seething pot began to boil over, and the sword rose up inside the house of David. The sons of David began fighting among themselves as to who would be the next king. A daughter was raped by her own half-brother Amnon, and his half-brother Absolom had Amnon killed over the incident. Absalom, raised an army against his own father and was slain by Joab, David's commander-in-chief of the armies. These iniquitous deeds committed by David and the standard set by them continued on through the house of David much longer than three or four generations. Nearly every generation after David acquired and perpetuated these iniquities so that the sword continued upon the children (subsequent kings) of the house of David, up to and including Jesus.

The second prong of the second deed was that David conspired to murder and thus was guilty of transgressing the sixth law, *thou shall not kill*. The punishment for killing another human being is death (Genesis 9:6). Some students **might interpret** that God had a problem with that punishment concerning David. Without knowing the God of the whole Bible, some might think (as I did at the beginning of my studies into the Perfect Law) that is why God overlooked the punishment of death and let David live. After all, David was in God's long term plan for the nation. He was God's choice of Kings over Israel (1Sam Chap. 16) and His purpose for David had not yet come to a conclusion. But considering that God can raise up children of Abraham from stones on the ground (Matt 3:9, Luke 3:8), I would like to suggest this situation did not pose any dilemma to God. God was ready to **allow** David to die for his transgression, iniquity, and deed. The important word here is **allow**. God would have allowed the Perfect Law to perform as designed and return death upon David for his deed of murder.

Surely God would have had an alternative to David if He had needed one. Omniscient God had no other. God knew David, and He knew David would repent.

In the past, while teaching Bible study classes, I have often asked the question, "Have you ever heard of Miz-Rahb-El?" Of course no one had; Mizrahbel is a figment of my imagination. Continuing on, I create the story that Mizrahbel was never mentioned in the Bible even though he was God's first choice to deliver the Israelites from Egypt and to receive the ten commandments. Because Mizrahbel was too busy complaining and doubting there is a God, God chose an alternative. It was Moses. The lesson is designed to show that God always has someone in the wings to carry on.

When Elijah was afraid and running for his life from Jezebel, he complained to God that if he was killed there would be no one left to worship God. I can only suggest God's laughter was heard throughout Heaven. God informed Elijah that He had seven thousand in Israel who had never bowed their knee to a false god. (1 Kings 19)

I am encouraged by the way the second deed of this narrative of King David did unfold, because there is mighty truth contained about the forgiveness of God toward those who have committed **heinous crimes**. Though the punishment was death for anyone who kills another, the scriptures inform us that David **immediately** understood his iniquity, trespass, transgression, and deed, as well as who these were committed against. There was but a millisecond between the time of David's realization and his confession. True repentance was immediate, and God was there to forgive and deliver. David declared, *"I have sinned against the Lord."* Nathan **promptly** gave the verdict, *the Lord hath **put away thy sin; thou shall not die**. However, because by this **deed** thou hast given great occasion to the enemies of the Lord **to blaspheme, the child also that is born unto thee shall surely die**.* (2Sam 12:14)

I embraced an important principle I had seen before only in shadows. That principle is how God deals with our most wicked iniquities, trespasses, transgressions, and deeds. No matter how very evil they may be, all can be forgiven and erased if confession is made with a sincere act of repentance. David knew his sin and recognized it was not against Uriah that he sinned. David trespassed Uriah, and he trespassed Bath-sheba as well their unborn children, but David's transgressions and the iniquitous sins that caused them were against God, and God alone.(Psalm 51 was written by David concerning these incidents with Uriah and Bath-sheba.) When David confessed this with a broken and repentant heart, he was forgiven of the iniquity, the trespass, the transgression, **and the deed** he had created. David did not die as a result.

Nathan immediately had words in his mouth as though he had been previously informed what David would do and/or say. This, I suggest, is an example of omniscience on the part of God (Amos 3:7). It also tells us God was looking upon the heart of David to know he meant what he said and that he truly was repentant (1 Sam 6:7). Nathan, it would seem, already knew the verdict.

This one recorded event in David's life is so very important to realize. What it says in effect is that no sin against self, no transgression of the law, no trespass against a neighbor is too big for God's loving kindness not to forgive **both sin and deed**. God's loving kindness is **always unconditional**, and His forgiveness is always according to our repentant heart.

Two deeds done—murder and adultery. One was forgiven and notably dealt with as forgiveness. The other was returned to David in multiples. In both cases, **something sowed was reaped**. David sowed murder and would have reaped death, but realized his iniquity and **over-sowed repentance**, which reaped forgiveness. David sowed adultery and reaped the same—only more. A pattern was emerging, and I was beginning to define the parameters of the Perfect Law. That one scripture in Galatians kept returning to me each time I saw a similarity between what was done and what was returned. *Be not deceived; God is not mocked: for whatsoever a man soweth, that shall he also reap* (Galatians 6:7).

The third and final deed of David had me working overtime. I had assumed that the cause of the death of the child born out of the adulterous act had something to do with David's causing the death of another. After meditating through 2 Samuel 12:14 word by word several times, I realized this child was not put to death due to David's conspiracy to commit murder, but because by the deed, David had given the enemies of God a reason to despise God. **God had forgiven David's sins** of conspiracy to commit murder and God had **removed the deed that would return** to David as a result of that transgression. The fact before the court now involved only this child's future. David's sin had given the people a reason to blaspheme God, and this child was the evidence of the transgression. The mere existence of the child would serve as a reminder of David's iniquities and give the enemies of God a reason to murmur against God for many years to come.

I need to introduce another story from my own past to defend the taking of the life of an apparently innocent child. Forgive me if that makes it sound like God's wisdom needs defending. That is not my intention as His will needs no defense. It is my intention to show there is more than one side of this story: the story as told through David's eyes, and the story as it might have been interpreted through the eyes of this child. I pray my story will help some of you who have lost a little one prematurely by seeing one of the reasons why God **allows** it. Keep in mind that death is a human reality. Death is not viewed in God's Kingdom or in eternity or by God in the same way finite humans view it. To a humanist, death is dispiriting. By Kingdom's definition, it is part of the process of life; it is merely a door we go through to move on.

Early in my Christian experience, a grandson of a man who helped to raise me was killed in an automobile accident. It happened on the way home from church camp when the church van he was riding in went out of control. The other passengers in the van had some nicks and scrapes and the driver broke an arm. Only one child lay dead.

When I first heard of it, I began to ask God, "Why?" As I was passing through the doors of the church for the funeral service, that still, small voice of God I was just learning to hear, spoke a few simple words into my heart. He said, "The child is not here; he is with Me." I mentioned those comforting words to the person with me as we took our seats.

This child's name was Chris. Chris was only seven years old when he went home to be with his Lord. During the eulogy at his funeral, the pastor spoke about the church camp and about that fate-filled time. He told the audience that during the last night at camp, Chris shifted uneasily in his seat, listening to the story of Jesus. He acted as if he had ants in his pants. He was waiting as patiently as he could for the minister to ask if anyone wanted to pray to have Jesus come into his life. As soon as the minister gave that altar call, Chris ran forward to give his life to the Lord. He was the first to hit the altar on his knees.

I knew this child was with the Lord. The Lord had spoken those words into my heart. But because I was the equivalent of a toddler in my own Christian experience, I was unable to fully appreciate why this happened to such a young person with so much to give and so far to go; why now, just at that point when the spark of God hit the fuel of zeal? I should have been born in Missouri. I am always asking God to "show me."

A couple of weeks later, I was in the end of town where they laid this young boy's body to rest, so I stopped to pay tribute at the grave site, intending to use the quiet time to fellowship with my Lord. Instead of quiet time, I was met by his mother and grandmother. They were joyful, smiling, and talking together as they placed flowers on the grave site. They were excited to see me. They wanted to tell me the story of how Chris, on the eve of leaving for the church camp that weekend, had asked his mother what it meant to have Jesus alive inside. He said he was going to the camp to find out and that He was going to ask God to let Jesus live inside him. The night before Chris left for camp, he and his mother knelt and prayed together that God would help him find the way. Both mother and grandmother went on to explain that after the funeral until that moment, nearly thirty people had given their lives over to the Lord as a result of Chris' testimony and what they saw God doing through him. It was then I realized the purpose for this child's life.

Several months passed before God answered my question and enlightened me as to the reason for Chris' early departure. It was a scripture in the book of Isaiah, chapter 57, verses 1-2 that God used to show me. It says, *The righteous perisheth, and no man layeth it to heart: and merciful men are taken away,* **none considering that the righteous is taken away from the evil to come.** *He shall enter into peace: they shall rest in their beds, each one walking in his uprightness.* I understood that some of us are taken home early because we will not be able to withstand the evil that will come upon us in the future. Only God sees our future (omnipresence), and only God knows what actions we will choose down the road (omniscience). For some of us (those who are right with God, which includes children before the age of accountability and all those who have made their commitment to God), God is merciful to deliver us from our future situations. God knows that some of those situations will be extremely painful and unbearable for our frail spirits. He knows that some of us will experience situations that will bring shame and perhaps a fall from grace, a fall from which we will never recover. I would like to suggest that when we come to this crossroad, rather than let us continue on to experience the worst one can experience, merciful God who loves us, knows best, and has promised to never push us beyond our capabilities (1Cor. 10:13), concludes our earthly ministry. In other words, our purpose for being here is finished. God allows the good to die young. Because life does not end at the death of a body, we must consider that God allows the righteous to be delivered from the evil to come and to enter into peace instead.

In the light of this personal event, I knew in my heart that no matter what came of David's child, the Lord's hand was in it for the good of the child, the "church," and of all those concerned. (Rom 8:28) Still I went back to the drawing board to further research God's law concerning the death of David's child. It was in this subsequent meditation that I realized David's actions were iniquitous, resulting in a murderous deed. This sent me back to Exodus 20:5. The iniquities of the father would be visited upon the children (compare Ex. 34:6-7). Upon further meditation, I realized the pain this child might suffer at the hands of the "media." By his birth (2Sam 11:27- it was a boy) and his presence in the kingdom of David, as he grew there would be great occasion for the enemies of God to blaspheme, doubt, and talk negatively about God and about the child, leading others to do the same. The damage done was twofold. 1 It would cause the child to suffer continually. 2 It would cause others to walk away from the God David served. Though David was forgiven, the deeds he committed lived on. As best I can align the scriptures, I suggest this child was delivered from the aftermath of David's iniquities, spared from future injustices, and allowed to graduate early to go home to heavenly festivities.

We have only a few recorded verses in scripture of the times David attempted trickery against Uriah. I suggest he made many unrecorded excuses, both before and after the event, as to why Uriah had to lead a battle against the strongest, most protected wall of a city under siege. Surely any seasoned veteran of the military would have spotted the danger and suggested a better way. David not only plotted, he caused others to plot. David's many selfish and intentional sins became iniquitous.

God declares Himself a jealous God (a "relative" attribute, so mentioned for our understanding. God's jealousy is for our protection. He wants us close to him and not associating with Kosmos ways. This attribute is akin to our human nature declaring "self-survival" selfishness to protect the place where our spirit dwells). According to the Bible, we are to seek Him and no other God; not Baal (a god of nature in ancient times); not Mammon (riches or wealth); Not little i am. God calls us to choose His way, not our own way. If by making a selfish choice we miss the mark of His calling upon us, it is okay. The real harm of a sin is only to ourselves. Confess the sin, make corrections to erase any deed, and move on. Do not repeat the disaster or try to cover it up. If you do, it becomes an iniquity. And if God has a purpose for you that has yet to be fulfilled, if by your own actions and deeds you cannot or do not expunge your iniquities in your lifetime, then God, by the Perfect Law, will be *visiting the iniquities of the fathers upon the children to the third and the fourth generation of them that hate me;* (Exodus 20:5) The child born of the iniquitous lies and conspiracies of David was visited. This child, by his death, was relieved of the burden of carrying David's iniquities into his own adulthood. The Perfect Law would have been a just and impartial executor of David's evil iniquity upon the innocent child as he grew to manhood, but instead, God was a loving God to **allow** the child to be relieved of that burden. Might I suggest my own interpolation of 2 Samuel 12:14: "Because by this deed the enemies of God will be speaking negatively about God for years to come and about the little boy who is the product of all of your foolishness, God is going to spare the young child the pain you have released into his life and gather the lad to himself for safe keeping."

Three deeds resulting in three punishments. Something went out; something was returned. I began to see the Perfect Law for what God designed it to be. It governs the liberties of man and records what we do—our works or deeds, both good and bad—and multiplies them back upon us accordingly.

How perfect a design to eradicate evil and reward goodness. This law delivers judgement and punishment or reward, all according to our own works, born out of our own free-will choices, and does not impugn Deity in any way. God needs never to change. In order to be merciful, allow us free will, and free Himself to love us unconditionally, Sovereign God chose to set a spiritual law in place, a governing law in between God and man that we, and we alone, control. **God took His hands off and left us to our own devices and desires.** He gave us dominion!

God was merciful to give us a manual (the Holy Bible) to explain that dominion. In that manual He alludes to a bottomless pit at the end of an evil road that selfishness places us upon. God has posted many signs along the way that say, "Do not do this. Do that. Walk this way." God has designed a Grim Reaper for those who refuse to listen. It is the Perfect Law, and it is waiting on the other side of those posted signs. We avoid becoming prey to the Law by choice.

Still we blame God for so many of the ills of our world, not realizing that it is the Perfect Law of Liberty set into motion before time began, that juries every event. We look at God and ask, "How could You?" We write "Acts of God" into our insurance policies and our professional contracts suggesting He is the cause when disaster comes our way.

My friends, God set us as lords over our own paths. We are free to choose, invent, explore, discover, experiment, and create. We have a total free-will. There are no parameters on our liberty. But beware: the apostle Paul told us that all things are lawful, but not all things are expedient (1Corinthians 6:12;10:23). That means that not every one of the liberties we choose will deliver us to a wonderful place. **Not all liberties are free.** Some liberties are liberating, delivering prosperity for good deeds done. Negative or selfish liberties when taken, will **always** exact some personal cost. When we choose selfishly, what we choose can return to do damage to ourselves or to a loved one. Selfish deeds will return in some form or another to exact an equal or greater worth, from the person or persons who, by their liberty, created them. If not them, then from their children, or their children's children.

God is free to love us. His unconditional love stands guard over each of us, weeping with us in our pain, rejoicing with us in our glories, and always ready to remedy any sour situation in which we find ourselves. He is always waiting for us to ask for His help. Then and only then can He step in to deliver us. And He will if we have not placed ourselves in a laughable position (Prov. 1, esp v.26).[2]

Initiated by this one narrative from David's life, I began to realize how formidable is this Perfect Law, what it is, and how it works. I began to see that what comes upon us is only what we bring upon ourselves, with few exceptions (which we shall discuss later). This crack in the mystery of God began to unfold to me, and for over twenty years now, the Perfect Law has been a rudiment in my ministry and teaching. It is time for the bushel to be taken off this candle and to let the light of the Perfect Law shine forth (in the spirit of Matt.5:15-16). Before we do, however, let us review some of the details I have spoken of thus far in our reading.

So far I have addressed perfection in three different ways: 1 Perfection of God, as in God is perfectly complete and needs nothing; 2 The perfection of the Perfect Law, a law designed to deliver promise or exact punishment perfectly; 3 The perfection of man, as in David was perfect in God's eyes, and did nothing wrong all of his days except concerning Uriah the Hittite. To this last example we can add Genesis 6:9 that states Noah was a just man and **perfect** in his generations. Genesis 17:1, God called Abram to be **perfect**. Deuteronomy 18:13 and 1 Kings 8:61, God calls the nation of Israel to be **perfect**; 1 King's 15:14, King Asa's heart was perfect; 2 Kings 20:3, Hezekiah had a **perfect** heart; 1 Chronicles 12:38, all the men of war had a **perfect** heart; 1 Chronicles 29:9, The people gave with a **perfect** heart; Job 1:1 and 2:3, Job was a perfect man. At this juncture, further discussions of the words *perfect* and *perfection* (in reference to man), are necessary; also of a new word *S/spirit* that I have coined and use in the treatise.

NOTES

1. There is a lesson here for persons involved in industries that might cause the children of others to stray from truth, God, or even the teachings of parents. The negative deeds produced that cause hurt to the child of another will come back upon the producer or his children, grand-children or great grand-children.

2. Take note of Proverbs 1, verses. 5,7,18,19,23, 24-28, 29-31, 32, & 33. These are all examples of the Perfect Law at work. I reported that this law was difficult to see because it is not mentioned by name. In this one chapter, we have nine examples of the Perfect Law at work—not by name, but by attribute and action. Learn to spot the Law in scripture and we will see it is alive and calling to us for recognition more than any other message in the Bible, except for the theme of the Christ.

Chapter 9
S/Spirit and Perfection

THE S/SPIRIT

In my writing, I will sometimes employ the term "spirit man," using a peculiar spelling—S/spirit man. This spelling is intended as a reference to a man who is united with God and on the road to perfection. The Bible teaches in 1 Corinthians 6, in particular verse 17, that when we join ourselves to God we become ***one spirit with Him***. Before this, man is guided primarily by his human nature. Once a man makes the decision to allow God to rule in his life instead of his own selfish human nature, God places the fullness of His Own Spirit into that man, which awakens his spirit and the two join themselves together as one. We then speak of the man as being a Spiritual human being as opposed to a natural human being. When I write, I entwine the spelling of the words with that idea, and enjoin the Spirit of God to the spirit of man in a word. The words resulting are "S/spirit," or "S/spirit-man," as opposed to natural man or fallen man (human beings, operating primarily from humanistic ideals). In like manner I also enjoin this idea to the employ of other words in this series. For example, God and I are O/one; The Godly accomplishment is O/ours. These words are designed to reveal a spirit in union with God.

PERFECTION

This road to understanding the Perfect Law had many potholes for me. I am not one to pass over or leave those potholes untended, especially when some are so obviously disturbing. In the study of David's life, we find gaping holes in his righteousness before God and in his service to Him as he fell from grace many times. Yet David was still considered by God to be perfect, an apparent and blatant (dichotomous) contradiction. I considered that perhaps my needle of interpretation needed to be repositioned in my board of understanding. My inquisitiveness compelled me to find the Biblical definition, or better yet, God's definition for Perfection.

In order to define what a Perfect Man might be, I had to look to our example, Jesus, for both testimony and teaching. Because He is the Son of God, Jesus is considered by Bible scholars to be the "perfect" man. According to scripture, Jesus was the fullness of the Godhead in human form (Col 2:9), but He was a man like you and me (Luke 2:40, Heb 4:14-15). The difference is that He was S/spirit man and understood the true reality of God. He was perfect and stood blameless before His Father in that He did only the things He saw His Father do (John 5:19-20;. Compare to 2Kings 15:5 *turned not aside from any thing that God commanded him to do.*).

During His earthly ministry, Jesus brought to our attention that we too should be seeking to obtain that same perfection in our lives. *"Be ye therefore perfect, even as your Father which is in heaven is perfect"* (Matt 5:48). Jesus gave this commandment **to the living** with **no allusion** to perfection being accomplished **only after** death. The fact that others, such as David and Noah, are called perfect men verifies the truth that perfection is attainable by mortal men before we graduate into the kingdom beyond, and that it was achievable even before the birth of Jesus. In other words, this event is not a "Jesus gave me the power to do it" thing.

Over the years, I have asked dozens of pastors their interpretation of Matthew 5:48. Very few have ventured outside of commentary. Most agree with the commentary interpretation explaining that the original Greek, the language from which our New Testament is translated, does not render the same definition of the word *perfect* as do our modern dictionaries. The Greek word for *perfect* merely means "to be complete."

So, let us all be *complete even as our Father which is in heaven is complete.* Even with this change in words, the ideology still seems unreachable. We must ask ourselves: Did Jesus come to make fun of truth? Did He come here to mock us? Was His grand purpose on Earth to laugh at our shortcomings and lay burdens on us that we could never hope to attain? Of course not.

I suggest that if **Jesus commanded me to do something, He must also have empowered me to perform it or known that I already had the power inside of me to perform it.** God never tempts us above that which we are able to overcome (1 Cor 10:13). When He calls us to a task giving us the will to do something, He also gives us the power to perform it (Phil 2:13).

Through years of study, I found that perfection is an attribute of S/spirit man. Perfection is attainable in this life as a result of knowing God (Matt. 6:22-34). It was also attainable by man even before Jesus came

S/Spirit and Perfection

(Job 1:1, Gen 6:9, Gen 17:1 The same Hebrew word "tamim" is used in these verses and in Psa 18:30). We do not seek perfection however, if we perceive the achievement of perfection as impossible, or if we have been misled in our understanding of perfection and how to master it.

When Jesus called us to be perfect, He called us to be just that. But perfection by Biblical definition is **"completeness"** *according to Godly design* and has nothing to do with the idea of *supreme, without fault or defect.* In other words, Biblical **perfection is accomplished according to specific purpose. The call to perfection is the call for each of us to be the person we were designed by God to be to the best of our abilities.** Jesus called us to be true to our own design, just as God is true to Himself. That is our "likeness" to God (Gen. 1:26), and it is a calling to each of us to find our specific purpose on the Earth. I was not called into God's kingdom so I could be changed into the likeness of Billy Graham, or Ghandi, or you, and vice-versa.

Perfection occurs over the course of time. It is a process accomplished by loving the Lord God *with all thy heart, with all thy soul, and with all thy mind* (Deut. 6:5, Matt 22:37, Mark 12:30), and seeking Him as if you were looking for a buried treasure (Prov. 2:4). In this accomplishing process we not only come to know God, we also come to know who we are in relationship to Him. Therein we find our specific purpose. The most accepted definition of perfect is defined by Webster's dictionary as *entirely without fault or defect: meeting supreme standards of excellence: flawless.* To perfect something, according to Webster's dictionary, is to bring something to a state of supreme excellence: rid of faults or drawbacks. This kind of perfection is unattainable by man. Only God can reign supreme, and only God can be perfectly and completely flawless. We can never attain His Godhood, as there can never be two Supreme Beings. Perfection, according to the Bible, can be defined as fulfilling our God designed purpose. This necessitates knowing God and knowing who we are in relationship Him (Matt6:33). Biblical perfection *is* attainable by man.

Jesus was a perfect man in that he completely fulfilled his purpose according to God's design on His life (Heb 10:9). His mission was to carry out God's purposes for His life as they were designed in eternity before the foundation of the earth (Prov. 8:22-38; John 17:5), and to do so, perfectly. Jesus' mission included living His life with an attitude of heart that loved and served God completely (Rom 15:8). Jesus was born a mortal man like you and me (Luke 2:6,7). To those who saw Him, who walked and talked with Him, He was the embodiment of God's love and truth. He was perceived thus because He was perfect. His life was lived out from designed perfection (John 17:4) with every attitude of His heart constantly set toward God, completely (John 5:19). When we, like

Jesus, acknowledge God as our Lord and the Designer of our life, and all other life (Prov 16:9), and seek to know God and to know our purpose, which is His purpose in us, and to fulfill that purpose through our own life as He has designed it, then His truth will begin to become our truth, and we, too, will have begun our journey into perfection.

Perfection is not only a stage of maturity to be obtained in so many years, it is also an attitude of the heart that can be realized this very moment. Consummating this attitude is not a "religious decision" to be a better person. God, who looks on the inward heart, looks only at the desire of that heart to know Him (Prov. 17:3 Heb 4:12, 1Thes 2:4,). Perfection begins when we realize there is purpose for us and for everything in our world, that there is a God who is above all we see and know, and that He is the Source of all things and our Source. When we realize we must be connected to this Lord of all creation in order to be complete, and then petition God for His help, He places us on our road to perfection (Heb 11:6). Our place in the perfection process is procured merely by laying self aside (believing God and considering God's way to be more important than our own) while asking God to do His work in us.

Perfection is a process to be followed through to completion, but perfection is also a point in time when the process can begin. When we first enter college, we immediately claim we are college students although it may take us years to complete all of our college courses. The college mentality and our student rights exist from the first day we enter that college even though we are only students and might not even know where our classes are or the names of our professors.

Likewise, when we realize our need for spiritual perfection (achieving our purpose according to God's specific design for us), and ask God to begin this work in us, we enter into the perfection process. It is at this point we become "perfect" students in God's "College of Perfection." God now works in us to bring about the changes necessary for our graduation from the perfecting process into the perfect person.

BLAMELESSNESS

At the moment we are accepted into His perfection process, by His grace we are also made blameless. A thorough study of the overall Bible text will teach us that God searches the heart of a person to know them (Prov. 21:2). He knows what the heart is feeling and is not influenced by the outward appearance of the individual such as the clothes he is wearing, the language he is using, the alcohol he is abusing and so on (1Sam 16:7). In other words, when we enter His College of Perfection, God does not judge our ability to enter according to any physical or worldly criteria. God looks on only the attitude of desire in our heart

S/Spirit and Perfection

to know Him and to be in His college. He does not require that we first better ourselves by giving up alcohol, drugs, sex, or even taking a bath or washing our hair. When we enter His College of Perfection, God accepts each of us into the classrooms **just as we are**, and **continuously defends our right to be in those classrooms for as long as we are there to study to know Him.**

God has always had His hand on us.(Job 12:9-10; Prov. 16:9). Before we knew Him, He was guiding our lives (Job 31:14-15; Ps 22:9-10, 139:13-18). By making suggestions to us through the Teacher in us or around us, God has been orchestrating our successes and failures to bring us to enlightenment. (Deut. 31: 20-21; 2 Chron. 36: 22-23; Jer. 10: 23; James 1:2-4). When we finally do recognize Him and ask for His design to come upon our lives, we are accepted by God into the perfecting process, and all of our past failures are forgiven and forgotten (Psalm 103). Immediately we are given a scholarship to His Perfection College, and we begin the process of perfection.

Upon enlistment, we find our God is a loving and caring God. He does not hold us accountable for our **ignorance** of Him or our **ignorance** of Kingdom Law anymore than we would be accountable for the knowledge contained in a midterm or final exam the same day we first enter college. Throughout our tenure, however, he calls upon us to understand Him and to learn Kingdom Law. During these days, we are cloaked in a love God calls blamelessness (Phil 3:6, 2 Pet 3:14, other readings Matt 12:5, Luke 1:6, 1 Cor 1:8, Eph 1:4, Phil 2:15, 1 Thes 5:23). This blamelessness allows for **mistakes of ignorance** (we are not expected to know God's truths immediately) and prevents our falling away into judgement (Acts 17:30; 1John 3:6,9).

Freedom from accountability is our "free ride" or our "get out of jail free" card. Blamelessness excuses the spiritual components of corruption (sin, iniquity, trespass, and transgression) when performed out from ignorance, and is provided by God's grace for our protection. Blamelessness **will continue as long as we stay in Perfection College continuing our education concerning God.** As we progress in our studies of God and Kingdom Law, blamelessness is systematically repealed to make us accountable for our actions in the areas of things learned. This process is exactly the way we raise our children. When children are born, they know nothing. As parents we would never expect our newborn babies to be able to feed and clothe themselves. Once they begin to grow and become more self sufficient in these areas, the provisions of Mom and Dad are systematically repealed (Acts 17:30b).

Let us take a closer look at blameless perfection by viewing the maturation process of one of history's greatest heroes. For this study we will reenlist King David. The Bible offers candid illustrations of some of the greatest failings by God's people. King David was no exception. Listed here are just a few of David's shortcomings.

David, after being anointed by God as the next king of Israel, entertains false gods within his own home, disobeying God's first commandment as defined in Exodus 20: 3-6 (1Sam 19:11-13).

David, after being anointed King by the High Priest over all Israel (1Sam 16), and after defeating Goliath by the "power of God" that he knew would protect him (1Sam 17), finds himself living in fear and running for his life, unable to believe God. Inwardly, David was denying all he had experienced of God. He sought help from a priest in the priest-city of Nob. He told this priest various lies, stole for himself God's holy *shewbread*, and took some weaponry from the temple. David then trusted in the weaponry that he himself had proven had no power against Godliness (Goliath's sword), declaring "there is none like it" (1Sam 21).

Because of these lies by David, the entire priest town of Nob is destroyed and all of its innocent inhabitants are killed (1Sam 22:6-19).

David runs from God's protection within his own homeland, believing he can hide from Saul among his enemies in the city of Gath. Gath was a Philistine city and the home of Goliath. Upon seeing his folly, David feigns insanity to escape (1Sam 21:10-14).

Later, David commits adultery with Bath-Sheba and has her husband Uriah killed so he could take Bath-sheba to be his own wife. (2Sam 11-12).

Considering just these few incidents from David's life, let us read God's testimony of David: *"Jeroboam . . . walked in all the sins of his father* (Nebat), *which he had done before him: and his heart was not perfect with the LORD his God, as the heart of David his father* [great-great-grand father, here interpreted more as ancestor]. *Nevertheless, for David's sake did the LORD his God give him a lamp in Jerusalem, to set up his son after him, and to establish Jerusalem: Because David did that which was right in the eyes of the LORD, and turned not aside from any thing He commanded him all the days of his life, save only in the matter of Uriah the Hittite."* (1Kings 15:1-5) In other words, David did no wrong **in God's eyes**. What David did do was within the Lord's design for his life. David accomplished his purpose with a heart that loved God and sought God's will for his life, except, when the Lord told him not to kill Uriah. All of the spiritual components of corruption performed out of ignorance while he was in Perfection College went completely and totally unjudged, **spiritually**. That is **not** to say the Perfect Law had no effect in the matters of David's physical deeds, only that spiritually these mistakes were not held against him.

Now compare that to God's testimony of Amaziah in 2 Chronicles 25:1-2. *"Amaziah was twenty and five years old when he began to reign, and he reigned twenty and nine years in Jerusalem. And his* *mother's name was Jehoaddan of Jerusalem. And he did that which was **right** in the sight of the Lord, but **not** with a **perfect heart**."*

Amaziah reigned as king and consciously tried to do everything right, according to the book, following all of the laws of the scriptures and the laws of the land (church and state as he understood them from human reality). In God's eyes, however, Amaziah had failed to be perfect. Why? I suggest because he did not fulfill the calling or purpose for which he was created **with a heart toward God**. His deeds were **right**, but his **attitude of heart** was **wrong** (Prov 21:2, Prov 24:12). His love for God and His attitude of heart to know God were lacking. Amaziah wanted to do everything right; he just could not give God control or recognize that God was in control.

The Law of Blamelessness **does not give us the right to do evil or wrong**. Perfection is established by seeking God continuously even though we experience **ignorant** mishaps. Once we **understand** God's truth and **understand** the way of our design according to that truth (as opposed to merely hearing meaningless words and attempting to apply them like a salve to the problem area), there is no excuse for choosing evil (doing wrong by choosing to serve self over God). Study the scriptures in Hebrews 10:26-29. *"For if we sin WILLFULLY **after that we have received knowledge** of the truth, there remaineth no more sacrifice for sins."* No excuse, so judgement must come upon the sins, iniquities, trespasses, and transgressions that we willingly committed. In other words, once we come to know a Kingdom Law, or the Godly way we should react to a situation, there is no more free ride in that area of expertise. We have learned it, we should know it, and now we must begin making right choices about those things God has taught us. God does not have another Son. He has no other sacrifice up His sleeve to cover over our stupid choices, and there are no "do-overs." So if we ignore what He has taught us, we will find ourselves facing the justice of God, just like those who have never entered Perfection College. Our blamelessness in the areas of things learned is gone, and we are made accountable by the Perfect Law.

Verses 27-29 of Hebrews go on to say that judgement **will** come. The Perfect Law **will** prevail. Those who ignored the warnings of Moses died without mercy because they ignored not only Moses' teachings but those who came after him. The rules God gave the people through Moses included curses if the rules were disobeyed. Moses recorded those curses in the books of the law, Genesis through Deuteronomy. How much more the punishment will be for those who willfully ignore God's truth or who hear the Teacher, understand the Way, and then **WILLFULLY** tread Truth under foot? Willful sins are performed **in spite** of the Spirit of Grace, that conscience Voice that lives inside of us and is guiding us to do right. Willful sins are never considered blameless.

Chapter 10

The Constitution of the Perfect Law of Liberty

God is infinite perfection. He is flawlessly complete. Fallen man, on the opposite end or opposing side (Psalm 2), is imperfect. By his own choices, he is and remains broken off from true Spiritual enlightenment. He is far from Godliness, living in God-denial, trying to find his way to success in his humanistic world by relying on his own selfish, human imagination and the machinations of others like himself. S/spirit man is somewhere in between fallen man and God. Having understood there is something greater than himself, S/spirit man has reached for that Divinity from a broken awareness and has begun to grow spiritually. As he grows and his knowledge of God is blossoming, S/spiritual man is granted blamelessness even though he often falls from the ladder of Godliness en route to perfection. In order to govern mankind fairly and deliver equality to all men, God instituted the Perfect Law.

BILATERAL LAW

Thus far, we have established the attributes of a law as universal, absolute, transcendent, unprejudiced, and incessant "workers," doing what they were designed to do. The Perfect Law has all of these, however, there is an additional attribute of the Perfect Law that gives it uniqueness. That attribute is bilaterality. The Perfect Law is bilateral, allowing it to work in opposite directions. The Perfect Law can be both positive and negative. It is the attribute of bilaterality that makes the Perfect Law an equalizer.

Bilaterality allows the Perfect Law to work for us or against us, to take from us or to give to us. Unlike the law of gravity which demands what goes up must come down, the Perfect Law allows men to "go up and stay up" or "go down and stay down," and each direction works independently of the other. If we could control gravity bilaterally, we would have no need of airplanes.

Bilaterality is the attribute of the law that allows us to use the Perfect Law as a tool. By our own choices we control what the Perfect Law does for us or against us. If laws had brains or could choose or judge, we would have no control. But like gravity, the Perfect Law does not think. It works perfectly, without passion or prejudice, to do what it was designed to do. The Perfect Law cannot and does not have any choice in any matter it oversees. It only observes what we do or what we give out and guarantees to return to us that which we do or give.

Let us look at an example of how we might use the Perfect Law as a tool. Stealing is a choice I make. If I choose to steal, my deed requires the Perfect Law to be just and fair to return my deed to me. I will be robbed in return, and I am guaranteed to lose more than I gained. According to the Perfect Law, I will get only poorer by choosing this road of destruction (Prov. 13:21).

On the other hand, bilaterally, if I choose not to steal, using the Law as a tool in a positive direction, then my deeds require the same Perfect Law to be just and fair and ensure that **no one can steal from me**. God, without changing, making a choice, or entering into the events of men, will, by the power of the Perfect Law, disrupt any attempt, make known any plot before it occurs, or catch any thieves attempting to steal from me. Failing these three examples, should a robbery occur anyway, then I am assured the goods, or an amount equal to or better than those goods, will come back to me one way or another. Why? Because I do not steal, the Perfect Law is obligated to ensure no one can steal from me (Prov. 12:21).

Let me lay this out as a scenario so we might better see how such events have occurred in our lives without our realizing them. I do not steal, so, according to the Perfect Law, no one can steal from me. Still, a man manages to take ten dollars worth of candy from my candy store while I am not watching and appears to get away with it (Jer. 23:23-24). When the thief gets home later that evening, his wife informs him their washer broke while she was doing laundry earlier in the day. The thief calls a repairman to fix the washer, and the repairman charges him a hundred dollars (Prov. 13:22; Eccl. 2:26), an amount ten times what he stole. On his way home from repairing the thief's washer, the repairman gets an unusual urge to stop by my candy store and buy seventy dollars worth of candy, something he never does, has never done, and might never do again (Prov 16:9). The amount is seven times what was stolen from me. In addition, unbeknownst to me, my own washer is granted an extra year of life by the Architect of life.

Who was rewarded? Who was punished? This is the scenario described in Proverbs 11:8-9 *The righteous is delivered out of trouble* (my ten dollars was given back in abundance), *and the wicked cometh in his stead* (it was taken away from the thief) . . . *through knowledge shall the just be delivered* (God will foil the plans of my enemy, or make known those plans to someone in position to change the events before, during, or afterwards).

We often fail to realize why the appliances in our homes continue to work far beyond their years or why we and our children never need the services of a dentist, a doctor, or a hospital. The reason is, the Perfect Law is returning goodness to us according to our good deeds. Vice-versa, the reason our car is so often in need of repair or our cash flow is so short may be the results of the negative side of the Perfect Law.

When we find ourselves struggling day after day, year after year, we need to take account of our lives. Where are we in the perfection process? What are we doing that is cause for our lack of prosperity? What deeds can we sow in our own favor to change our future?

Selfish deeds can be so trite they go without notice until they come back upon us negatively. Maybe we took that staple gun from our work place, a stapler that did not belong to us, and that is the reason the car splashed rainwater on our expensive coat that is now ruined. Or maybe we parked in a parking zone dedicated to a retail store we did not intend to enter in order to save ourselves time getting out of the concert down the street. By robbing a shop keeper of the parking spaces that he rents to ensure his paying customers have a place to park when shopping with him, we guarantee we will likewise be robbed, losing money or time someday in our future. How many of us roll right through that stop sign at the end of our street, ignoring the rules, then wonder why our own children will not listen to our rules? No matter how subtle the offense or the good deed, the Perfect Law works and will return it upon the doer.

Our negative deeds may be so subliminal we forget or fail to take notice. HA! Do not deceive yourself. We take extra care to look both ways long before running that stop sign at the end our street. We want to make sure we avoid an accident while disobeying that law. We know what we are doing! If we have not selectively quenched that consciousness inside us that tells us right from wrong, we know when we are not doing what we should be doing. So, do not deceive yourself! God will not be mocked! What you sow, you will reap!

Let us consider one more example. This one has become a pastime for some of our young people, and they have no idea they are hurting themselves by it. Stealing music downloads or intellectual material off the internet is robbing the artist of his income and stealing food from his and his children's mouths. Young people must not deceive themselves! Their day is coming when they might have an invention, patent, book, or song, the royalties of which they might depend on to feed their children. Parents, we need to teach our young people that honoring the work of another guarantees others will honor their work. Their actions while they are young will keep a competitor from stealing their territory or their job when they are older. We always need to treat others as we ourselves want to be treated.

THE GOVERNOR

Only the wisdom of God could find a way to fairly, equally, and justly govern the chaos of fallen man and S/spirit man living side by side (Matt 5:44b). Consider that two men are standing side by side performing the same act. They are both giving the same amount of money to a needy child. Each will receive a reward, but each will be rewarded differently. The first man, a S/spirit man, because his heart was right toward God, sees the suffering of the child, and, guided by his S/spirit, does what the Living Spirit of God inside him is guiding him to do to relieve the child's pain. He is rewarded. Within a short period of time, twice the amount of his gift will be returned to him in some way or another. The other man, a natural or carnal man, is one who is separate from God and not attentive to God's will for his life. His heart is motivated by little i am. He gives his gift, but his motivation and desire is that the S/spirit man and others see his good deed. As a result of his attitude of heart, natural man's gift is **not** returned to him in abundance. According to the teaching of Jesus, this fellow has already received his reward—to be seen of men (Matt 6:1-24).

Only God could design a way to make our motivations transparent and a law to give to every man his just due. God did this by designing the Perfect Law. Into the Perfect Law God designed two central guidelines: 1 The Law looks upon the **deeds or finished works** of a person to **reward or punish** that person; 2 The Law looks upon the attitude of the **heart** of a person to **judge** the person. The result is that rewards and punishments are delivered justly and fairly by the Perfect Law. Judgement is taken out of the care of God and placed squarely upon man. Every man and woman in every walk of life everywhere is personally accountable to God for him or herself.

The Perfect Law governs the events of men in this way: 1 It returns to the doer of a deed what the doer put out through the deed; 2 What and how the Perfect Law returns that deed is determined by the **attitude of the heart** of the doer. For instance, if a selfish deed was performed out of vengeance, God's Perfect Law will return that deed upon the doer (1); the amount of vengeance with which it was delivered will determine the force with which it will be returned, as well as the content of that returned deed (2). Likewise, if a Godly deed was performed out of love, God's Perfect Law will return it upon the doer (1); the amount of love with which the deed was delivered will determine the force with which it will be returned, as well as the content of that returned deed (2).

From our scriptures in 2 Samuel 11 &12, we can see that all of the tenets of the Law are present in the discourse between King David and Nathan (2Samuel 12:5-6). *And David's anger is greatly kindled against the man; and he said to Nathan, As the Lord liveth, the man that hath **done this thing** (deed) shall surely die (deed return). And he shall **restore the lamb fourfold** (deed restoration equal or greater), because he did this thing, and because **he had no pity** (attitude of the heart).* Deed and attitude are both present, as well as compensation.

For the purpose of teaching, I have named the judgement according to the attitude of the heart our ***Standard of Measure.*** The Standard of Measure represents the demeanor by which the Perfect Law returns the deed. This is a standard we ourselves set by our attitude of heart. I draw this term from Luke 6:38 which says: *Give, and it shall be given unto you; good measure, pressed down, and shaken together, and running over, shall men give into your bosom. For with the same measure that ye mete withal, it shall be measured to you again.* This scripture promises that if we give, it will come back to us. But it also tells us that with the measure we give it, it will be measured back to us. Simply stated, what we give will be returned according to the attitude (of the heart) in which we give it, or the Standard of Measure we create for ourselves when doling it out (Jer. 17:10 ways **and** deeds are measured). The idea behind this and similar scriptures is the principle that good always begets good, but how much the good is to be multiplied and how it is to be returned **depends upon the attitude of heart** with which the good was delivered. If we give begrudgingly, it will come back sparsely. If we give with a cheerful heart, intending to truly give (not expecting anything to return), it will come back in abundance (2 Cor. 9:6-12). The attitude of our heart is **our** choice and becomes the standard by which the return is determined for each particular deed.[1] Although the scripture in Luke 6:38 is most often applied to money, the principle according to the Perfect Law applies universally across the board. Whatever we do, or give, or sow will be returned to us. It is this principle that allows **the Perfect Law to be used as a tool** to bless us and bring us good. If we give love away, love will come back to us. If we want to have a friend, we must be one. If we are looking for Mr. or Mrs. Right, we must concentrate on becoming Mr. or Mrs. Right; only then can we give Mr. or

Mrs. Right (ourselves) away. When we give Mrs. Right away, we will get back Mr. Right. If we give away a broken, uncaring, baggage-holding, vindictive, God-insensitive Mr. Wrong, guess what we will get back? If we care for others, others will care for us. If we want people to be polite to us, we need to be polite. If we want the people around us to be thoughtful, we must be thoughtful. Do we want respect? Do we want people to quit gossiping about us? Then *as ye would that men should do to you, do ye also to them likewise* (Luke 6:31). Whatever you put out, it will be returned to you. *Judge not, and ye shall not be judged: condemn not, and ye shall not be condemned: forgive, and ye shall be forgiven:* (Luke 6:37).

Likewise, if we do not cheat, we **cannot** be cheated. If we do not lie, we **cannot** be lied to. If we do not steal, others **cannot** steal from us. According to the Perfect Law, whatever we put out—good or bad—will come back to us. This is not to say that others will not try. Have you ever been in a position when you knew someone was trying to lie to you? Have you ever had that sense that the person you are dealing with is trying to cheat you? The Holy Spirit, your teacher, will tell you through your conscience everything you need to know. The more you know of God and the better versed you are in hearing Him through the language of Bible, the more your receiver, tuner, antenna, and speakers will be working to receive His warnings.

The Standard of Measure collaborates with the Perfect Law and regulates the measure of the returned deed. If we give with a willing and open heart expecting nothing in return, abundance will return. If we put something out with anger or begrudgingly, it will lack abundance when it is comes back. The Perfect Law assures us that what we sow, we will reap. The Standard of Measure assures us that how we sow it will determine the temper as well as the quantity of that returned deed (2 Cor.9:7).

The book of Romans, chapter 12 has a whole different context when read in the light of the Perfect Law. The key verse, verse 19, reads . . . *Vengeance is mine; I will repay, saith the Lord.* I suggest this scripture might be interpolated "Vengeance is mine saith the Perfect Law of the Lord." In other words, we need not worry about someone getting back what they put out. If they do not seek forgiveness and make compensation, the Perfect Law guarantees it will return to them more of the same in the same way. If not to them, then to their children or to their children's children to the third and fourth generations. Revenge or vengeance is not our problem. These are not ours to deliver. Vengeance can become our problem should we choose to make revenge our Standard of Measure. We should learn to let go of any malice done against us. God will right every wrong by the Perfect Law.[2]

The Bible tells us to pray **for** our enemies (Matt 5:44), not **about** them. God will take care of those who come against us. He will return to them double, ten, a hundred, or even a thousand times what they put out and push them back toward the path of His design for their life. Asking releases God to work as a second participant, a partner to the ruler who asked, to deliver dutifully, bountifully, and immediately the Perfect Law to work.

When we ask, God may allow the Perfect Law to work immediately. Bear in mind, the Perfect Law does not need to be invoked by the prayer of man. It will mosey on by itself. But any ruler on Earth can use his or her dominion power to ask God for help, authorizing God to participate. When God is enabled, He cuts to the quick and empowers the Perfect Law to work immediately; angels are set into motion to minister—to halt any wrong in progress or to bring about the return of a blessing, immediately! (Daniel 10 esp. v2-4 & 12; 2Kings 19:8-37)

If we do not ask God to help, the deed will still return, but it will come by way of due process. Such a return may take time. Such a return may take a lifetime. By asking God, we release our dominion to Him and He is free to enter into the events of men and make corrections immediately. If we ask for help, help will come. This is salvation to the spiritual! But beware and be ready! If we pray with a judgmental heart for God to "fix" a person or a situation, we are also praying for ourselves. That is the way the Perfect Law works. If we are praying because we judged another as unworthy or we think our way is better, we may be the ones outside of God's design (Romans 14:4). God will bring about the necessary change, but He may do so by allowing the Perfect Law to go to work to change us. The Perfect Law does not bless evil or evil intent from anyone. It will only punish it.

The Perfect Law is a blessing to anyone for whom you pray it. It speeds up the returned measure to the doer of good as well as the doer of evil. The blessing to the doers of good is obvious. It blesses the doers of evil by bringing these prodigal sons closer to knowing God's hand is upon them. God sees what they have done, are doing, or are about to do, and will deliver justice. There is but one way to escape His wrath. Only God can protect us from the wrath of God. (Ps 11; Prov. 18:10) They must right themselves before God or they will be made right by God and the Perfect Law. (See Prov. 25::21-22, Romans 12:20-21). Our prayer is simple. *"Lord bless _____ according to your Perfect Law. Let your will be done on Earth as it is in Heaven."*

The Perfect Law is a perfect law. It does not impugn Deity. Sovereign God, by Sovereign choice, set the Perfect Law into motion to act of its own accord on His behalf. Deity is outside of the courtroom of human reality. Reward or punishment is delivered to each of us by the Perfect

Law, according to our own works and by the attitude of our own heart. The Perfect Law has no mind. Like gravity, it does not think or despair. It acts as it was designed without partiality or prejudice. **Man is in charge of his own destiny**, and God is separated from any judicial action. Judgement is set forth by the Perfect Law designed to deliver to man his just due. God is still in control of His universe, but is relieved by the Perfect Law of any adjudicating interaction. God is then free to interact with unconditional love, to deliver and to bless His creation **when He is called upon.**

Finally, I must add, that blessings upon the doers of evil can result from our verbal warning. I spoke with a young lady recently who was having problems with her son hitting other children on the school playground during recess. When asked for advice, I quickly summarized a portion of the Perfect Law and advised her to share it with her son. She did, and the following day, her son disregarded the warning and pursued his normal bullying tactics anyway. This time, he was met with resistance, pushed down, and injured. His own words to his mother that evening were, "I got back what I did."

This young lady's child would never have known "he got back what he did," unless he was aware of the Perfect Law. When mom spoke it into existence, it became a living entity and entered the mind of her son, enabling his spirit to see, acknowledge, accept, and appreciate the "judge" and the judgement. He will utilize his new knowledge to guide in future decisions because someone made him aware.

NOTES

1. As a side note, I might add that God and the Perfect Law see only the genuine attitude of the heart. If we give because we are supposed to give, or if we give expecting nothing in return because that is what the "law" of the Bible demands, our return will be sparse as though we gave begrudgingly. The attitude of our heart must be genuine. S/spirit man does only what the Spirit of God in Him is doing according to the 'nature' of God. A river does what it was naturally designed to do. It does not have to plan to flow downstream or think about obeying the law of gravity. It neither navigates its course, nor does it labor to achieve its designed purpose. A river rests in God's design for it, and does what comes naturally. Likewise, the man of God, the S/spirit man, does what his S/spirit genuinely, naturally guides him to do. It is not a rational choice to obey a law, but rather like a reaction, a knee-jerk response to what is set before him to do and is performed without a second thought. The beauty of the Perfect Law is that right becomes so ingrained in the man of God, that all our responses in righteousness become like knee-jerk responses. If we meditate in the Standard of Measure, we will see it is God's perfect safety measure. Because it reads the attitude of heart, the Standard of Measure prevents evil from using the Perfect Law to any benefit (Prov. 28:5).

2. This return upon the children is not confined to returning only after the death of the doer of the iniquity. Watching our children suffer because of our poor choices can be a part of the punishment for our deeds in this life if we do not repent and make compensation. I fear this is the plight of many innocent people who are falling prey to earthquakes, tsunamis, whirlwinds, floods, and so on. Any **innocent** victim that has bound himself, by his religion, to a wayward sect of that religion, a sect that uses violence and promotes death to anyone who does not believe exactly as they do, is in harm's way. Such wayward sectarians will punish even their own brothers and sisters and have no conscience toward unconditional love or the forgiveness it demands. There is but one God who is called by many names. He is the same God of the same Abraham who fathered Moses and Jesus in his lineage. Almighty God IS Unconditional Love. He does not kill and likewise demands the same of us. The innocent need to stand up and separate themselves from those who take the law into their own hands. Until they do, they will continue to share the punishment of the deeds returned upon the wayward—death for death, but more of it—by war, by earthquake, by tsunami, and so on.

Americans are not exempt. America recently lost a city that was embroiled in corruption, crime, and hedonism. This city drew its very life and its sustenance from the deeds that are defined in Bible language as an abomination to Godliness. Sodom of the Bible was destroyed for all of those same reasons. The iniquities of the fathers came back to fall upon the innocent in Sodom. Those who died may have been personally innocent, but bound themselves to the evil of others. Time does not change God because God does not change. God made the rules for the people in ancient times, and those same rules remain intact today. God gave man dominion power. It is our job to seek God out, know His ways, and find His truths so we know how to use our dominion power properly. He warned us not to deceive ourselves; to deny His warning is to mock Him, and He **will not** be mocked. He told us we would reap what we sow. He told us when we ignore him He would allow the **storm** and the **whirlwind** to devour us. He warns us that if we ignore Him, He will ignore us and will not hear us when calamity comes and we cry out for help. The Perfect Law works! (Proverbs 1:20-33, 1 Chronicles 28:9, Isaiah 46:9-13).

Chapter 11

Mastering the Perfect Law of Liberty

To know and understand the Perfect Law is to have mastered it. That is the simplicity of this Law and a testimony to the wisdom of Godly design. We need no more than to see how it works and what it does to begin employing it. Learning the basics of the Perfect Law is akin to learning how to fish. The basic elements of fishing are very simple and involve a hook, some string, and bait. We learn to employ these elements by testing and trying them out at the fishing hole and refining and enhancing the experience each time we visit. Our desire will determine the successes of our experiences.

Like learning how to fish, once we understand the basics of the Perfect Law, we can take the Law to the fishing hole of life to begin testing its tenets. The results achieved from employing the Perfect Law vary according to free will and individual choices, determination and desire. Our experience with the Perfect Law will cause our understanding of it to grow, and we will ascertain for ourselves what this Law has been to us, how it has already affected our life in the past, and what we must do to make positive any negatives caused by our ignorant misuse of it. Learning the constitution of the Perfect law will help us to realize that if we have stolen thirty times in the past, we must un-steal thirty times. If we have lied fifty times in our past, we must un-lie fifty times to undo the damage. We will soon deal with the various ways this can be accomplished.

Handing someone this book or telling them about the Law in a thirty minute lesson will not likely teach them all they need to know about the Perfect Law. With the Perfect Law, experience is our teacher, and each of us will have our own experiential-learning interim before we can cause the Perfect Law to work for our good. For some, it may happen immediately, but for most of us it may take some time. Most will have to meditate on the magnitude of the Perfect Law to realize how personally significant it is and how it has already affected our lives. Regardless, we can begin to utilize it right away. The Perfect Law is not like an exercise program that we have to study, build ourselves up by continually working at it while hoping for results, and finally, should we achieve, continue struggling in order to maintain. Quite the contrary. Once we understand the Perfect Law, once we comprehend its value, the difficult work is over. Our mind and our heart will not be able to unlearn it, un-employ it, or ignore it. We will not be able to forget it or forget to use it. The Perfect Law, already in our spirit, will enter our conscious mind and the Teacher in us will begin to use it immediately to guide our every future decision and action. In time, using the Law successfully as a tool will become a part of our character. We will no longer have to think about using it to make the Perfect Law work for us.

Using the Perfect Law correctly from this point forward and using it to undo any past damage will result in a positive flow of prosperity, relationships, health, and so on. Every avenue of life will change for the better as the infinite attributes of God's Spirit are enjoined in us. These become our attributes through our commitment to seeking God and knowing Him and His ways (Matt. 6:33). Among these attributes are love, joy, peace, long-suffering, gentleness, goodness, faith, meekness, and temperance (Gal. 5:22).

Using the Perfect Law adversely once we understand how it works is difficult, but it is possible. Guided by selfishness, one can underachieve by the power of this Law and by errant choices that ignore its consequences. But even those who choose the negative will, by the very same Law, find themselves in a place that will force them to rethink their decisions. I suggest this is one of the subjects of the story Jesus told of the prodigal son (Luke 15:11-32). The Perfect Law has a way to correct the worst in us.

Not knowing the Perfect Law does not make this Law or any law go away. It is still in effect and, like gravity, is working for us or against us, depending on how we address it to our everyday experiences. If we want the Perfect Law to work for us, we must use it positively. It will work against us if we use it negatively or try to ignore it altogether. Consider the effect the law of gravity would have on us should we ignore it altogether and walk off the cliff, believing the law to be powerless. If we want to **make** a law work for us, first we must know it exists, then we must understand how it works, and then we are free to take dominion of it for benefit.

Our understanding of the Perfect Law does grow, and our experience with the Law is enriched as we realize how the Law has and is affecting us and everything around us. Once we understand the Law, we will be able to spot it in operation in our everyday events and the everyday events of those around us. As we learn to recognize the Law at work, we will gain a sense of control by knowing why an event occurred. We will be able to determine what caused the event to unfold the way it did, boosting our confidence about the dominion control we have of our own future. An excellent example of recognizing the law at work is expressed throughout the book of Job in the Old Testament, especially chapters 4, 5, 8,11,15, 18, 20, and 22. In these chapters we can see the friends of Job describing the Perfect Law in operation. Job's friends knew the Perfect Law and were judging Job by it. They could not comprehend the real reason for Job's misfortune and suffering. This entire book of Job is much more comprehensible when read in the light of the Perfect Law.

Knowing the Perfect Law is working and that it is working exactly as it was designed will cause our faith to flower. We soon learn that when we apply the Perfect Law, like God Himself, it is always there for us. When we apply the Law positively, it will reward us every time. Because a negative application will return punishment upon us, our knowledge of the Perfect Law will make us contemplate, speculate, think, and rethink before making decisions. Knowledge of the Law will cause us to manage our choices more purposefully.

At first, the Perfect Law can be very captivating, but it can also be very frightening as we begin to consider all of our past negative deeds that might return to punish us. I suggest that fright is the reason man has kept his innate knowledge of this Law suppressed. The Law rewards goodness, but it discourages human nature's favorite pastime—selfishness.

As we overcome the negatives, reversing the Perfect Law's adverse effect on us, we will begin to realize by experience what this Law was designed to do. This Law was created to be a purposeful guiding force for good in our lives. We will also realize how the Law was designed to support good, deny evil, and level the playing field in order to make life equal and fair for everyone. The more knowledge we gain of how the Perfect Law is and has affected everything in our world, and the more we experience the Perfect Law and use it as a tool for our own good, then the more we will want to endorse it and employ it for our own good as well as the good of those around us. If we continually use the Law properly, without fail, it will take us to peace and prosperity. If we ignore the Perfect Law, the Law may work against us just as gravity might work against us if we choose to ignore gravity.

The most frustrating thing about the Perfect Law is that there is not much to know about it. As we begin to understand the constitution of the Law, we will become more aware of it. Then we will begin recognizing the Law in action all around us. As we recognize the Law in action, we will begin to acknowledge the Law really does work. When we acknowledge that the Law is real and does work, we will want to use it to our advantage. In order to use it best to our own advantage, we will want to know more about how the Law works, what it does, and so on. It is here that the frustration begins because there is nothing more to know. The Law is such a self-explanatory and elementary law that any knowledge beyond the fundamental constitution of the Law comes only by our experience with the Law. God created the Perfect Law to be that simple. It was designed to be understood equally by the most child-like mind and by the most knowledgeable, MENSA qualified professor. There is no Ph.D. in Perfect Law. Although *you reap what you sow* has ruled the world since the dawn of creation, it has always been simple to understand; so simple that it is hard to believe the events of our world could ever move in a negative direction. Everything happens for some reason. There is always a cause to every *why*.

We have and always have had the ability to employ the Perfect Law to work in beneficial ways. It is part of our dominion package designed by God and installed in our spirit as innate knowledge. I suggest the reason we little know and hardly understand it is that man has suppressed the knowledge of the Perfect Law over the course of time. The Perfect Law does not reward selfishness or the self-centered. I suggest it is mankind's propensity for selfishness, self-centeredness, and greed that has led to his ignorance of this all-important law.

The possibility to suppress the knowledge of the Perfect Law exists. It is possible to subdue any memory. Psychologists call this ability *denial*. The human mind was designed with selective memory, an ability to put away or set aside unpleasantness. An unpleasant sound, for instance the sound of freeway noise near our home, can be selectively repressed. Often times the mind automatically quells our most difficult memories, like an automobile accident where we or someone with us was seriously injured.

In this same way, when something gets in the way of a selfish desire—something like the Perfect Law—we can use denial to force the mind to ignore it. If we do so repeatedly, we can eventually suppress the knowledge of the Perfect Law. I suggest the fallen, human mind, controlled by choice to selfishly serve little i am, has suppressed mankind's knowledge of the Perfect Law over the past century. As a consequence, mankind is experiencing a world that appears to be out of his control. Suppressed for five or six generations, this Law is working against us instead of being the tool for success and progress God empowered it to be (Hosea 4:6).

To help us realize how little we respect and acknowledge the laws of our world, try this exercise for a few minutes. Sit back and contemplate some of the ways the law of gravity is working all around us where we are. We will see that gravity is at work everywhere in the place we are. Gravity is in control of every object in our vision. Gravity owns everything in sight, but, do we think about it? Although it does not make itself overly apparent, the law of gravity is always surrounding us, owning our environment. For instance, the world is spinning at approximately 1000 miles per hour, yet we are not flying off into outer space. Do we ever take the time to wonder why not?

If we do not contemplate gravity and what it is doing to aid or defeat us, we will never see gravity for all it can be. Our lack of attention does not undermine the law or disturb the existence of the law. Although we realize something is causing the things around us to fall or stay in place, without some consideration or academic study we will never discover to the fullest what gravity is, how it works, why it does what it does, and how it can become our tool. As a result, gravity will never work for us beyond our negative or positive happenstance experience with it. We will continue, as we always have, to accept the results of its attributes as it hands its circumstances to us. In this capacity, gravity is in control of us and our environment. The law of gravity dictates how we move and how our world unfolds. Without Sir Isaac Newton and all of his successors, we might still be riding buggies to Baltimore. Knowing any law and how it works allows us the control. There is no end to the possibilities.

The Perfect Law is a Law like gravity is a law. This Law was designed to be understood and used as a tool. Though we are aware of the Perfect Law by experience, so few of us understand the functions and the purpose of the Law. Even fewer have learned to use the Law as a tool. Everyone acknowledges the Law with choice phrases like *do unto others as you would have them do unto you* or *you will reap what you sow,* but the purpose for the Law was that we take charge of it and use it in a positive way. As a result, we will get back in abundance everything we put out. Only then can we determine our own destiny. We can succeed and prosper by the power of the Perfect Law.

Chapter 12
Some Necessary Sidebars and Notes

We are nearing the end of this discussion of the Perfect Law. We need only to cover the variants. Before we discuss those anomalies, I must take a few asides and attach a series of notes to what has been said so far. Perhaps I can assuage some who have become discomforted. I realize I may have stepped on principled toes to get to this place in this teaching, and I ask any who may have found offense to forgive me, be patient, and consider the entire book as a whole before any judgement is made. There is much more depth to these words than can be set forth in so few pages; however, I am trying to present these ideas in a way that those without a deep understanding of Bible knowledge or of the language can appreciate and find comfort or guidance. To all those who have a command of the Bible and its language I say this: The doctor does not come for those who have no need of medical care, but for those who are suffering from their maladies (Matt 9:12).

1

I must take the first juncture to defend the contradiction I created by saying God does not judge. This aside is addressed to any who were unsure of this assessment, although I believe it is those who have a strong Bible knowledge and are philosophically capable of arguing the dilemma who might disagree most. This message is designed to clarify those acts of judgement in which God **does** participate.

There are many scriptures in the Bible that speak to God judging us. I feel I have dealt sufficiently with most of these, explaining that change renders God incapable of judging. I further explained that God has put systems in place that allow for judgement without His direct interaction. I have used various scriptures to say that no one—not

Christian, not Hindu, not Muslim—is free from judgement at the end of time, and that God will judge us then. To align all of our needles in the board, we must now consider the scriptures that deal with God judging us at the *end of time*.

I have introduced the idea that God does not make judgements. If we study the Biblical text as a whole, we will understand how judgement is rendered and who it is that renders it. We will see that at the "end of time," it is the Lord Jesus Christ who will sit upon **that** throne of judgement (Matt.25:31-34; Acts 17:31; Rom. 2:16; 14:10; 2Cor. 5:10). This is His right as one of us (John 5:22-27). When the nature of God came among us, He became one of us (John 1: 1-18). He was born a man like you and me. The name of His humanity was Jesus. He was also recognized as the Christ or Messiah by some, and addressed as Lord by others.

Nowhere in the Bible do we find Jesus addressed as the Lord Jesus Christ until after He had earned that New Name by His death, resurrection, and ascension. That new name inferred that the man Jesus had completed His mission as it was designed. The manifestation of God who became the man Jesus had now ascended and returned to His rightful place as Lord of Creation. In that position, He is now both God and man. Only The Lord Jesus Christ, both God and man, is capable of fair and righteous judgement upon mankind. Let me say this in other words, and I say this very reverently; until God became a man and experienced life as a creation, He was "incapable" of judging creation with the fairness expected of a sovereign God; thus, the interim need for the Perfect Law. Now, because He is man and has experienced life as a man, He can and will judge man at the end of time. Because He is God, any judgement He renders will be just and fair.

Consider also, there is no "time" in eternity. Everything in eternity always is. God IS the beginning and God IS the end—all at the same time (Rev. 1:8). That is the meaning of omnipresence and the explanation of the Name of God—I AM—presented in Exodus 3:14. Omnipresence is not only the attribute of being everywhere present, but it is the attribute of being every*when* present as well. So, from eternity (God's viewpoint), the judge is already in His place and has been since before the world in our time began. Any dichotomy produced in the arena of judgement is the result of man's humanistic interpretation of God's reality and his inability to understand this concept of God's true reality.

2

By now, some scholars are qualifying this work as a type of Deism. I must also correct this misconception. Deists are those who believe in a detached God. Deists believe God wound the world up like a clock when He created it and then went away. As a result, the world has been running its own course ever since. Every religion has some piece of the puzzle, some portion of the truth, and this is the Deist's portion: God created the world and then rested and has been resting ever since. Resting, according to the Biblical definition, is not sleeping. It is a position or a station of love and awareness that is free from worry and fear. (The book of Hebrews explains this *rest* and includes God's invitation to man to enter into this *rest of God* with Him.)

Though I do believe God set this world into motion with all of its rules and laws, and checks and balances, I do not believe God then walked away. I believe, as the Bible says, God rested (Genesis 2:1-3; Hebrews, chapter 4). I believe God determined man would have dominion of the earth, and God determined He would not interfere in the affairs of men unless invited. Knowing man's propensity for selfishness, God knew man would wander outside of God's design, and create havoc that would need to be corrected. By establishing the Perfect Law, God disengaged Himself from entering our dominion uninvited to make those corrections. The Perfect Law would oversee and manage all of man's decisions to keep him on course, and to correct any course gone awry.

By His sovereign design, God would be free to love all of creation unconditionally and through the Christ or Anointing, lead and enable his commanders-in-chief to bring all of creation into designed perfection (1Cor 9:24-27, 2 Cor. 10:3-5). Make no mistake: God is Sovereign. Deity is and has always been in control, and can end our experience at any time.[1]

I hope through this treatise that I have properly presented a Sovereign God—One who chose to create the world the way He did and then give it over mankind to rule and run as man saw fit. God designed a way to help us with our experience without interrupting our dominion. He enters into our experience when invited. By this design, God is constantly and continually involved with creation; this is the result of those who are vigilant and doing their part by inviting Him in. It takes only one; praying the Lord's Prayer is a fine example of how a single person can change the world (Matt. 6: 9-13, esp. V. 10).

Those who lack the knowledge of the Perfect Law are running on apathy or selfishness. Apathy, like selfishness, is a choice. Apathy becomes our choice when we do not take a ruling authority over our own lives. If our world is in trouble, it is in trouble because the Perfect Law is doubling back to us everything we have ignored or selfishly put forth without a mind toward Godliness (Matt. 6:33; Matt 22:37).

3

Although the subject of this section is not a belief running rampant in the church, it is a common misconception entertained by many Christians, and I feel obliged to challenge this misconception in this treatise. The misconception is that Satan somehow obtained dominion over the earth during the fall of mankind. That is to say that by choosing self over God, Adam handed his dominion authority over to Satan. This idea is based primarily on two scriptures. The first is in Luke 4:5-6. In this scripture, the devil is offering Jesus the kingdoms of the Earth and all power which he alludes he owns. Jesus rebuked the devil with a scripture. Because Jesus did not refute the devil's claim, many believe the devil must have a right to that claim. To that I say, as Jesus did in John 8:44, The devil is a liar and the father of the lie. The devil did not deserve a response to this claim, only a rebuke for assuming a position he did not own.

In a second scripture, John 12:31, Jesus referred to the devil as the prince of this world. World, in the Greek language, is Kosmos, which refers more to a system than a place. The devil was the prince of the world system, or the prince of the un-God-ly way of doing things, not to be confused with having dominion over a planet. The same word, Kosmos, is used in John 14:30, and John 16:11.

Paul refers to the devil as the prince of the power of the air in Ephesians 2:2. This title refers to a spirit realm in which the devil is actively a participant; again, not to be confused with a planet. As evidence to man having dominion, we can use the beginning chapters of Job where it can be plainly seen that Satan had no power or dominion over Job or anything in Job's world except that which God would permit. God does not change and God does not change His mind. God gave man dominion, and David restates mankind's claim to that dominion in Psalm 8, nearly halfway through the recorded history of the Bible.

4

This aside is to sharpen our understanding that perfection is a process that cannot be properly judged apart from Godly knowledge and wisdom. Not one of us has any idea what God is doing to or with any one else. Nor are we aware of the timeliness of the events that cause any of us to walk toward Him. (1Cor 7:17-24)

When I was wandering through life, lost and searching, I asked the God I did not know to show me the truth and to let me know if He really does exist (Ps 145:18-19). I asked Him for this one full year before He presented Himself to me. Should I assume God just woke up on the day of my salvation to deliver me, having had nothing to do with the 365 days full of events before that day? Or could I assume he was preparing me for my day of salvation every moment of every one of those 365 days that preceded the event, as well as every other day since my birth? Anyone outside my circumstances might have looked at me and judged my plight as hopeless. Likewise, I am sure if men had formed a jury to try King David for all of his mistakes, the second half of the Bible would be different.

In the gospels we find Jesus teaching his disciples that just **because** a man does not say the exact same words or follow **our own** calling **does not mean** he is not doing the will of God (Mark 9:38-41). *For he that is not against us, is on our part.* (Every choice comes down to one of two ascriptions; God and Not-God.) Paul teaches us in Romans that where there is no law to guide, men become a (perfect) law unto themselves (Rom. 2:14), and they will be judged accordingly (Rom. 2:5-6). Our days are busy enough with their own evil (Matt 6:34). We should go about them with our yea as yea, and our nay as nay (Matt. 5:33-37; James 5:12). Since we do not know what the Father is cooking up among our neighbors and fellow brethren, it is best we stay out of His kitchen (Compare Judges 14:1-4, esp V 4). We need to concentrate on only ourselves and how we affect those we touch. I have three rules I live by, and these I push forward to everyone God allows me to influence them. 1 Do what is set before you to do day by day knowing it is God who set the task before you to be accomplished by you. 2 Do it to the best of your ability, using all of the God-given talents with which you were endowed, knowing if God gave you the task to perform, He also gave you both the will and the power to perform it. 3 Perform the task, and do it as though you were doing it for Almighty God Himself. Do you realize that if every cobbler made his wares by these rules, each of his shoes would be near flawless and fit for a king?

5

This aside is to address the idea that God loves us all equally. First, I must say to all non-members of the Jewish faith, there are no commandments for us but to love. The ten commandments and all of the rules laid down by Moses were Jewish laws designed by God to deliver the Hebrew people of old to the day of Jesus and to likewise deliver for posterity the Holy Scriptures in existence. Jesus did not come to Earth to resurrect the Jewish law or Judaism so it could be pushed forward into a new era. He came to be an example to us of how we should be as children of the Living God (John 13:15; 1Peter 2:21), to explain His place in the prophetic part of the Jewish scriptures (Luke 24:13-27; esp V 27), and to expound upon how His being the fulfillment of the those scriptures was designed to change the old ways of doing things and bring us all back to our original purpose and position in God (Matt. 5:17; compare Matt. 1:22; 2:15,17, 23; 4:14; 8:17; 12:17; 13:35).

In his teachings, the apostle Paul, a renown Jewish leader and teacher of Jewish law and history, told us that Jewish law could not deliver us from sin (Rom.7:12-14). Paul's book to the Romans explains that in our natural power, we are unable to do what the law demands of us. According to the oldest book in the Bible (Job), as far back as time goes, men knew that man is incapable of keeping God's law just as man is incapable of being God (Job 25:1-6). Only God can do such things. So, God devised a way to enter into a man and abide in him, to live in man such that His Holy Spirit becomes one with man's spirit and together they function as one S/spirit in one body (1Cor. 6:17). No longer is it me who lives alone in this body, but God's Anointing lives with me in this body (Gal. 2:20). The things that He does I am doing because God is wearing me around like clothing, and when He lifts his hand to heal, the sleeve of His clothing goes with it. The things He does, I do also (John 14:12).

The rules that once seemed so difficult to the Jews . . . *"Ye have heard that it was said by them of old time, Thou shalt not kill;"* appeared to become even more difficult to follow when Jesus came. . . . *"But I say unto you,"* (Jesus speaking) *That whoever is angry with his brother without a cause, shall be in danger of the judgment:"(Matt. 5:21)*. These newer rules, the truer intentions of God for man, are not really more difficult; they are only more difficult without God enjoined to us through the Anointing, the Holy Spirit living inside of us. The laws and rules of God are only arduous for man when he attempts to accomplish them on his own, but they are easy for the Lawgiver and Rule Maker Himself who lives inside of the S/spirit man and IS the Author and the Accomplishment of these rules and laws.

In the body of his epistles, the Apostle Paul expressed what happened to him when he ultimately understood the scriptures as God intended. In Romans chapter 7, Paul tells us the law made him realize his sin by making him aware of the lustful desires of his human nature. It was then Paul realized he had misunderstood the law as he had been taught it and had been living it his whole life. Paul had been taught he must live the law to be right with God. To live the law, one must perform the law and do the law completely. Until he understood God's true intentions for the scriptures, Paul had felt confident he had done all that was required, and he had adhered strictly to the commandments: Do not commit adultery, do not bear a false witness, and so on. But when Paul came face to face with the last commandment, *thou shall not covet*, and when he understood it as God intended it to be understood, he said it killed him (destroyed the old man in him). *Thou shall not covet* means thou shall not want or even **want to** do what the other commandments tell you not to do. Paul realized he had fallen short of

God's intentions his whole life, and he realized what he must do to effect the change and become one with his Creator. He confessed his weaknesses and asked God for help (Romans 3:23, 6:23;5:8-10;10:8-10,13). Only the Anointing of God inside a person can empower a person to do as God would do (Romans ch. 7-8).

Paul teaches us throughout the book of Romans that apart from God, man is broken off and separated from God. He has no direct access to the wisdom, truth, and knowledge of God. Man's actions, apart from God, can be only human, with total, humanistic (not-God), selfish intent. Man is a human . . . in the act of being. Even the words *human being* suggests a self without God. (A human *being like God* suggests the opposite.) If a man has quenched the Spirit of God in his conscience by his continual choosing of evil over good, self over God, he is surviving by only his fallen nature and a heart that may try to do right according to the book and the law-of-the-land, but not with the perfect heart required by God and witnessed by the Perfect Law.

Jesus addressed the Pharisees, the most rigid, dogmatic religionists of His day, teachers of the law and purveyors of all of God's recorded truths. He told them that tax-collectors and prostitutes would enter the Kingdom of God before they would (Matt. 21:31). Jesus looked at his own followers and warned them that unless their righteousness exceeded that of the teachers of the law and the best of Jewish hierarchy, they would not see the kingdom either (Matt 5:20). God looks upon the heart (1 Sam 16:7). It is the heart of a man that the Perfect Law sees and judges. It is the actions and intentions of our "perfect" heart or our "fallen," natural, human heart that will guide our life and prepare our future. We are personally accountable for ourselves.

The Standard of Measure looks on the heart and the **intention** of that heart in order to judge a man. The Perfect Law looks on the finished works or deeds of a man to reward him for the decision he made in his heart. In God's kingdom, anger is murder. Gossip is conspiracy to commit murder. Anger is a "want to." "I am angry with my neighbor. I **want** my neighbor out of my way so he cannot defy me. According to civil law, I cannot hurt him without being punished myself, so I will *kill* him with slander. Then others will see him for what he is and will also **want to** do away with him in their minds, bury him in their personal relationships, and have nothing to do with him." Essentially, by gossiping, one can kill without killing, but such deeds never go unnoticed or unpunished by the Perfect Law.

The Perfect Law is the glasses God is wearing. He is looking through them into the hearts of men. His eyes pierce through the veil of Christian, Jew, gentile, news reporter, black man, scientist, politician. He sees only the intention of the heart of Muslim, Buddhist, atheist, actor, Caucasian, lawyer, engineer. In the eyes of the Perfect Law, we are all the same. I might add, speaking to Christians—God is not blind to your selfish deeds just because you have the blood of Christ upon you. Oh, contrare! The following scriptures are just a taste of how God is going to deal with your deeds, born again or not. Remember I said: It is not important what **we think** about the deed or how **we think** God deals with the deed. God's design for the deed is the only importance. What is God going to do?

Romans. 14:10-12 *But why dost thou judge thy brother? or why dost thou set at nought thy brother? for we shall **all** stand before the judgment-seat of Christ. For it is written, As I live, saith the Lord, **every knee** shall bow to me, and **every tongue** shall confess to God. So then **every one of us** shall give account of himself* (his works or his deeds) *to God.* 1 Cor 3:11-15 *For other foundation can no man lay than that is laid, which is Jesus Christ. 12 Now if any man build upon **this** foundation* (a foundation in Christ—speaking here to born again believers), *gold, silver, precious stones, wood, hay, stubble; Every man's work* (deeds) *shall be made manifest: for the day shall declare it, because it shall be revealed by fire; and the fire shall try **every man's** work* (deeds) *of what sort it is. If **any** man's work* (deeds) *abide which he hath built thereupon, he shall receive a reward* (righteous deeds are tried by fire also). *If any man's work* (deeds) *shall be burned, he shall suffer loss: but he himself shall be saved; yet so as by fire.* Rev 22:12 *And, behold, I come quickly; and my reward is with me, to give **every man** according as his work* (deeds) *shall be.*

To the Christians I suggest, as the book of Revelation also encourages us, we should wake up and strengthen those things which remain (Rev. 3:2). Selfish Christians may be in trouble (Matt. 7:21; 25:31-46). Do not think anyone can hide from the One with whom you have to do (Heb 4:13 KJV). There is no evil done in darkness that will not be brought to light. (Luke 12:2-3, Num. 32:23, 1 Cor. 4:5). Look at your own life (Lam.3:40). The rest of the world is. We were told others can know who we are by our fruit (Luke 6:43-46). Prosperity is a promise of the covenant (Deut. 8:18). Are we succeeding (Joshua 1:8)? Are our children a testament to our fine parenthood? (Ps. 128; Prov. 20:7; Prov. 17:6). Is our life a testimony to the power of God? The whole world can see us. They are not reading our Bible. They are reading us.

Christians are all designed to be partakers of the great commission Jesus gave to his followers in Acts chapter 1, verse 8. He alluded to the fact that all of His Spirit-filled followers, those who were with Him then, and those yet unborn, would be witnesses for Him throughout the whole of Earth. I marvel that He did not say we would be good ones or bad ones.

6

Forgive me if I have ruffled some Christian feathers by announcing I was arguably adamant that understanding and employing the Perfect Law is enough to get us where we need to be to enable ourselves to find enlightenment as God has prepared it in the Christ and to enjoy this life in God's Kingdom here on Earth. My purpose was to present the Perfect Law through the history of the Bible. As a result, my words were carefully chosen so as not to offend my reader. I consider that although salvation is our experience, it is God's accomplishment in us. Our part in the development of our perfection is to be open and receptive to Him.

I ask any who may be offended by my offerings to carefully study all of my words and pray about them before making any judgements. In this way, you may avoid bringing the Perfect Law to bear down negatively upon yourself (Romans 14). Remember, I was called to this task whether or not anyone chooses to believe it. Remember also that I am not here to convert or convict or proselytize, but rather to share the message of the Perfect Law through the Bible as history. I have taken every step with great care to select these words, having devoted myself to much prayer and to petitioning the Spirit of God for help.

It would be most difficult for me to convince a man to accept my services as a clothier after telling him he has no fashion sense and that the clothes he is wearing look like they had been coordinated by a fool. The words in this treatise are not created for itching ears; they are words offered in love and in the hope of bringing those who might not otherwise listen because this message is presented through the Bible way.

To any of my brethren who have found offense I say: Take heed! Remember it is God who calls us, God who washes us clean inside, God who puts a new heart in us, God who puts a right Spirit inside of us, and God who sets us on our path. God—God—God. If I am to be an instrument in that process, I can only thank Him for allowing me the position, and prepare myself to be a string He plucks when He plays His chosen tune.

7

Young Bible students, do not confuse the Perfect Law or any of the physical or spiritual laws with the laws of Moses. The Law of Moses was a set of rules for good moral conduct, recorded to show people the way one should be if he or she is a child of God. When the Apostle Paul told us we were no longer under the Law (Rom. 6:14), he did not mean we were no longer subservient to gravity. Physical and spiritual laws are not laws to be obeyed in order to know God or to be morally correct. Laws like the Perfect Law and gravity are laws to be acknowledged and respected in order to succeed on Earth and in God's Kingdom on Earth.

The Law of Moses is like traffic. In order to get from point A to point B, one must become involved with and enter into the doing of traffic. In other words, we must load ourselves into a vehicle and follow the roads from the place we leave to the place we are going. The course is a plan with rules that must be followed. Traffic is a conscionable act of choice, management, and ability.

The Law of Gravity exists and is in effect even if we are ignorant of it or refuse to openly acknowledge and employ it. Our experience with gravity is just that—our experience. Beyond experience, we have little to discuss about gravity. Gravity is, and gravity works; end of story. We are involved in gravity, but it is not a conscionable part of our daily affairs. We learn to balance ourselves, walk, run, and climb trees by experience. Our reverence for gravity grows, but it grows subconsciously as our experience with it grows. We do not have to know about gravity, or study gravity in order to access and use it. However, if we do, we find great benefit.

8

I introduced the idea that God has but one perfect message, and that message is often confused by those who, for various reasons, lack the ability to interpret that message as God would have it. I want to diffuse any contention with this idea by expressing that even though God has a Way, and that Way is perfect, the Bible is designed to meet the needs of each of us as individuals. This allows for some leeway in Biblical interpretations. I suggest that we should not lose ourselves in the rigidity of dogmatism. God has a way of speaking specifically and personally to each of us through the words of the Bible. Those individual lessons allow for two or more of us to understand the same words of a Bible verse differently, yet those differences need not be misinterpretations.

None of us thinks exactly the same, so the stream of words used to combine a phrase for one individual's understanding might be different from the stream of words needed to reach another. For this reason, there may be many layers of understanding within a single verse. These many layers, however, will not allow for a mischaracterization of God or of the set principles of His perfection. In other words, no matter how many different ways we might read or interpret a single verse, each interpretation will align with the way and will of God. When an interpretation of a Bible verse fails to agree with God's perfect way and will, it has, most likely, been misinterpreted. Let me present an example to better make this point.

In a story Jesus told in the book of Matthew, chapter 25, verses 14-30, He spoke of a business man who was about to leave on a long journey. Before going, the business man pulled together three of his employees and put into each of their hands a sum of money to work with while he was away. Each had a different amount and each was free to trade it or invest it for the purpose of maintaining or increasing the holdings of the business man while he was gone.

The measure of money mentioned in the King James Version of this story is a talent. The exact worth of a talent varies throughout the Bible because the talent was a weight of metal. In some places, that weight might be 75 pounds of gold, in another it might be 132 pounds of silver. In every event, however, the talent was a weight of some metal and was considered a currency of the times.

Now someone reading this passage in our day might not read it in the light of history. If the reader does not have a Bible dictionary or a reference Bible with notes explaining what a talent was in ancient times, he or she might read the word talent and instead of currency, interpret the talent as an ability, like dancing or singing. If the reader is a dancer or singer, his or her mind might readjust other words in the text to fit more into their own personal understanding of an artistic talent, and may even use the idea of an artful talent when teaching this scripture. To a dancer or singer, an artful talent is personal and relative.

The idea expressed by either of these interpretations, currency or ability, is right. Both interpretations fit the idea expressed in the story Jesus told. Neither interpretation detracts from the way or the will of God. Though technically, one is a misinterpretation of the exact translation as it was presented by Matthew, it does not contradict the purposes of God. God has a way of using the many layers of a text to reach across the boundaries of our various understandings. In doing so, God makes the Bible personal and this kind of misinterpretation useful.

9

In chapter 8, I entered a footnote as a warning. In that message I said there was a lesson in King David's story for persons involved in industries that might cause the children of others to stray from the truth. Any negative deed produced that causes hurt to the child of another will come back upon the producer or his children to the third and fourth generations.

I have done my best to avoid editorializing throughout this treatise. This was done to ensure the message of the Perfect Law goes forth as clear and as precise as I received it. I do not want to hinder this message with my own opinions. I offer the following in a general manner and I hope it will be a blessing to all who read it.

Having studied the Perfect Law for many years and having assessed its character at work in the world, I have a reverent appraisal of the power of this Law. That power is frightening when it is released upon those who ignorantly pursue selfish indulgences for money or fame, not caring how others are affected. In America, these people often claim they have a "right" granted them by some amendment in our constitution, as though God Himself and His Perfect Law will be mercilessly disabled by some man-made law. The most frightening things I see are in the entertainment industries such as music, video gaming, motion picture, radio, and television.

If a song, video game, movie, radio or television show is produced that causes another man's child to stray from the truth of God, the producers are placing themselves and their own loved ones in harm's way. Those producers can be the financiers, the musicians or actors, the sound technicians, the album cover and poster artists, or the printers of such. Even those who package the product for shipment are in harm's way although their Standard-of-Measure-intent will not return so great a punishment upon them as it will upon those producers with an agenda to convert another man's child to their way. If the product causes another to stray from the truth of God, it is better that a millstone be hung around the neck and one toss himself into the deepest sea than to face God on judgement day (Matt. 18:6). If that music, video game, movie, radio, television show causes an injury or a death, a like deed will be returned upon those who had any part in making or promoting it. Promotion can be as simple as, "Hey friend, listen to this new album I bought." No one is out of reach or exempt from the equalizing power of the Perfect Law, absolutely nobody. That means, if a religious person produces a book or teaches a lesson that causes another man's child to stray from the truth, he or she may be causing his or her own children or his children's children to fall into the "hands" of the Perfect Law (James 3:1). Unless the components of corruption are disabled by repentance and compensated, the Perfect Law will always exact punishment upon the doer of any negative deed.

I recently saw an article concerning the Not-God agenda of a state university newspaper. This newspaper had published cartoons degrading the Lord of Creation, the very Son of God Himself. The proponents of the cartoons defended themselves by declaring their right under the first amendment to the constitution—Freedom of Speech.

When such things are brought to my attention, I trust they are set before me by God. He is calling me, as one of Earth's rulers, to intervene on behalf of these people. My asking allows God to move His unconditional love into that situation. The focus of my prayer is usually the ignorant people who might be sucked into evil in the vacuum created by the selfish indulgence of someone with a Not-God agenda. I pray—*Father, forgive the innocent. They have no idea what they are doing.* My prayer allows God to forgive any innocent person involved with this publication, and to begin to work in his or her life to bring about change.

I want to use this incident, if I may, to expound the possibilities of evil. To do this, we need to use our imaginations in meditation. I am going to paint a scenario of how such ignorance can affect our future. This exercise is not intended as an opinion. This is an example of how the Perfect Law **does** work. But it is my created story, which makes it somewhat an opinionated editorial.

A simple, Not-God cartoon degrading the Lord Jesus Christ fell into the hands of a young college student during the very time her decision to follow God was being made. It added to some of the other devises that had been confusing her about God and keeping her from walking toward perfection. This one picture, however, was the determining *straw that broke the camel's back.* The idea contained in the cartoon left such an impression that it caused this young lady to delay her decision about following God.

In the months that followed her missing of the mark, more damage was done by evil influences. She was introduced to alcohol and drugs, and her mind and decision-making abilities became even more clouded. Had she laid aside self to follow God she might be experiencing love, peace, and joy, but her mind had been influenced by a simple, degrading caricature of the Lord Jesus Christ. Now she was making the worst of decisions for herself, creating more and more pain and suffering as each day passed.

This young lady's life became a mess over the next two decades. Her drinking, drugs, and all of the problems resulting from her wayward choices shattered her family. It broke her mother's heart and put her mother in the grave, early. All of the pain she caused to her friends, family, and especially her mother, finally overwhelmed this young lady and she took her own life.

That simple cartoon degrading the Lord Jesus Christ was created by a liberal arts professor with a secular agenda. He liked his little i am life. One day, when confronted with a God above him, this professor was challenged to lay self aside or to attempt to eradicate the one thing that most intruded upon his little "i am" conscience—the righteousness of The Lord Jesus Christ. He decided to make a statement.

This professor drew a series of cartoons showing the *God* so many people revered, as a dubious caricature. He "knew" in his human heart there is no God (Ps14:1; 36:1-4), so there would be no repercussions to his actions. His actions were nothing more than fun and mind games. "It will make people talk," he said in his own defense, "It will bring about discussions, and the idea of God will be argued across the campus."

Now, twenty years after the publication of that simple, degrading cartoon, that same professor stands helpless over his own daughter's deathbed, watching cancer eat her body. The cancer, the doctor told him, is one of the slowest growing cancers. The doctor was surprised the cancer was so pervasive throughout her body. He suggested to the professor that the cancer probably began mutating many years before it was discovered in her. (About the same time the professor's caricature drawings of the Lord Jesus Christ began a terminal "cancer" in the mind of the child of another.) The professor watches his wife pray for their daughter, but he himself has no faith to believe in a God who would do such a thing to a beautiful, innocent, young child. End scenario.

Bear in mind, God did not cause the cancer or the good cells of this young lady to mutate. As she grew up with her father, she began to walk in all the ways of her father. According to the Perfect Law, wickedness breeds wickedness (Ps 58:3-5). There came a moment of decision in her own life when she walked out of God's loving kindness into judgement. There was a pit-bull sleeping under the rabbit hutch and no Godliness sown that might defend her. The Perfect Law had been used in the opposite direction by a parent, and he set an example for his daughter to follow.

If we have understood what has been presented of the constitution of the Perfect Law so far, then this scenario will reveal itself to us. This actual event became known to me through a news story as I was polishing these last pages for print. I invented this scenario to help me focus on the problem as I was praying for the innocent young adults involved. The printing of the degrading cartoons really did happen. The students attending the College of Journalism at this university were there only to get an education in journalism. They did not have an evil agenda or even a desire to degrade God; they had no intention to hurt anyone. They were merely innocent layout and page editors or printers, doing what they were asked to do for that particular publication. Because they made no protest or attempt to stop the publication of such material, they bound themselves to the event. May God have mercy.

This is just an imagined scenario of the workings of the Perfect Law. But I wanted to introduce it to say—Beware! Your own decisions today, no matter how simple you might imagine them to be, are making waves far into your own future. The deeds you create today will live long. The famous movie director Cecil B. DeMille is still touching millions of hearts in the 21st century with his positive movie, *The Ten Commandments*. Cecil B. DeMille died in 1959.

FINALLY

Learn the constitution of the Perfect Law. This Law is our judge. It can be our tool for success or the instrument of our own self-destruction. Everything changes when we understand the Perfect Law. The Perfect Law is indeed a law, and it runs and rules this planet according to man's free-will choices. The Perfect Law guarantees every human being will reap what he or she has sown. The Perfect Law guarantees that any human being, by his or her own choosing, can change his or her own future. When man, by his own choice, invites destruction upon himself, he can change the course of his own history by sowing what needs to be sown to effect a change toward the positive. That final outcome of every event has always been in the hands of some member of the human race. God designed it so that Mankind would have the dominion and the final say-so. He is without excuse. Man can navigate this life on his own using all of his human talent and knowledge, or through prayer, he can invoke the help of the Architect, the One who knows best, Creator God.

In order to petition the Creator's help, man must humble himself by realizing he is only a creation of He Who is All in All (1 Cor 15:28). He must realize his weakness, his **inability to be God**, and his necessity to relinquish his life and his circumstance to the only One Who can be God. Then he must *ask* God to do what needs to be done. This is the beginning of our humility, and it leads to our finding our own perfection. *If my people, which are called by my name, shall humble themselves, and pray, and seek my face, and turn from their wicked ways;* **then** *will I* **hear** *from heaven, and will* **forgive** *their sin, and will* **heal** *their land.* (2 Chronicles 7:14)

Read Proverb 1:22-33. You will see that God is out of the judgement/punishment loop, and the Perfect Law is at work, ready to deliver the whirlwind to those who trust in their NOT-GOD *isms* (V.31). God is here for creation in a purely loving capacity, waiting to grant deliverance to those who recognize him, truly repent, and ask His forgiveness (2Peter 3:9). Without recognizing God for who He is or honoring Him for our very breath, the destruction we bring upon ourselves will come and will punish. God says of these hearts that are hardened against Him that He will laugh when calamity and dread comes upon them. (Prov. 1:26)

Let it be known, the reason the righteous always win in the end and the reason evil always fails is that the Perfect Law works. NOT-GOD adherents will never understand this principle. They will fight adamantly to present the idea that the Perfect Law is a ruse. They will do what they can to try to destroy and bury any knowledge that thwarts their selfish i am desires. By not acknowledging the Perfect Law, these NOT-GOD people cannot use it as a tool. The Perfect Law will only work against little i am principles of selfishness to deliver destruction. NOT-GOD people cannot succeed against the Godly. They only bring the powers that be to bear upon themselves, their children, and their children's children.

Look again at David and all he did to himself by the Perfect Law. The Law was about to deliver punishment for the death of Uriah, and God, by his own Sovereign design to let David have dominion of his own life, **could do nothing**. The Law was in place, and the Law is blind as to whom the perpetrator of the Law might be.

David recognized his sin and he recognized that his sins were against God and not only against Uriah. He recognized it immediately and sought forgiveness from the only One who could grant forgiveness. God knew the outcome before it occurred because God is omniscient, but every angel assigned to David was wringing its robe in anticipation.

God was waiting with unconditional love to deliver to David what He wills for us all—forgiveness, rest, love, joy, and peace. God was prevented from delivering any of this until He was asked by the one in charge of his own situation. Like King David's future, our own future is in our own hands. That is bad news for some. How unsettling that can be! We do not like that! It is much more comfortable being the victim. To blame someone for all of our woes and attempt to wrest some reparation from them is much easier. No matter how I feel, no matter what I think about it, my future is my fault. My problems today are caused by my actions yesterday or by the actions of one of my predecessors. Nevertheless, I have the ability to change even that, so **my** problems today are according to **my** own choices only. Life is designed to be fair.

The good news is that God's love broods over us like a mother hen over her chicks (Matt. 23:37, Luke 13:34). He is waiting to forgive the man impounded by his own negative standards and to deliver any man at any time from the constrains placed upon him or that he has placed upon himself by the power of the Perfect Law. God has no need to oversee our world. He gave it to us to do that. He has no desire to judge, reward, or punish. The Perfect Law does all that for Him without conscience. Because of the powers entrusted to man and to the Perfect Law, **God remains neutral**. Consequently, God does not see man as man sees himself. According to God, there is no Jew, no Buddhist, no gentile, no black, no white, no male nor female (Gal. 3:28). There is only humankind—in need of God.

By the power instilled in the Perfect Law, God is free to love everyone equally without prejudice. It is the Perfect Law that prosecutes, juries, judges, eliminates evil, and encourages good—all without prejudice. We regress or progress according to our own personal accountability. We hold the reins of the vehicle that has promised to take us where we desire to go. Man is master of his own fate. He has been master of his own fate ever since God gave him dominion over his world.

The design is perfect. Evil comes back upon itself to destroy itself, if not in this generation, then in generations to follow; evil comes back and will eventually wipe the slate clean of all evil doers in every iniquitous line. Likewise, love begets love and grows. Contrary to Chicken Little, the sky is not falling. The Bible tells us there was a time of old when **every** thought, and **every** imagination of man was **only** evil continually (Gen. 6:5). There are not as many lions in the jungle today as there once were. God, by the Perfect Law, is eliminating the ravenous. If we look around us, we will see it happening locally.

NOTES

1. See His power over man by the Perfect Law in 2 Chron. 16:9; Ezra 8:21-22; A note should be made here that the philosophy of Deism is devoid of the Christ. Diests do not believe in the Christ. There has been a great claim by humanists in our modern day that many of the Founding Fathers of America were Deists. There were a few, but I suggest we review the journals and papers of these men before making any judgements. The writings of most will disclose a close personal relationship with and often mention of the Christ and of the Lord Jesus Christ.

I would also suggest we consider the direction in which the United Sates is moving away from God and more toward secularism. The Founding Fathers of America, when they wrote the words, life, liberty, and the pursuit of happiness, meant the *liberty* I am speaking of in *Liberty—The Perfect Law*. They understood this law as I am presenting it. Their writings and their well-documented history will bear this out.

Chapter 13
The Advocate

I had a devil's advocate while I was preparing these pages, a strong Christian and learned student of the Word. She wanted to know if there was ever a time when the Perfect Law was not in effect. The question was, "Are a Christian's deeds sometimes overlooked because they are Christians?"

I asked, "Does God sleep?"

"I don't believe He does."

"Does God wink His eye at sin and let it pass?"

"Of course not."

Then I asked, "When a man trespassed a brother in the Old Testament, was he by law permitted to pretend it never happened?"

"No."

"Not even if the trespass was in ignorance?" I continued.

"I don't think so."

"When a man ignorantly killed a neighbor's cow in the Old Testament, why do you suppose he was required to replace it?"

"I never thought about it," she said,. "I always assumed it was the law."

"I suggest to you that law was God's way of teaching us deed cancellation," I informed her. "Canceling out a deed prevents it from ever coming back."

"So, no matter what the deed or the intention of the heart, it will come back."

"Negative deeds are guaranteed to return to us in one form or another until they are erased. Positive deeds will always return to bless us. Our religion, or lack thereof, doesn't matter. The Perfect Law can't see."

"What about the man who accidently pulls out of a side street in front of a speeding car he did not see because it was going so fast, and the speeding driver is killed. Is the man accountable for murder?" She asked.

"Was the intention of his heart to murder someone in that instant?"

"No," she replied. "It was an accident."

"Then he is responsible only for a death, an accidental death, but yes, he is responsible for that deed he helped create."

"But it was not his fault!"

"Ah!" said I, "So he was not really there driving, and he did not pull out in front of the speeding car."

"No," she replied. "He was there, he just wasn't paying attention, and it was an accident."

"If he was driving, responsible for the vehicle he was in, should he not have been paying attention?"

"Well, yes, but sometimes you can't be aware of everything."

"Perhaps not, hence the term, ignorant mishap."

"So he is not responsible," she surmised.

"Was gravity working throughout the accident?"

"Of, course."

"Why?" I asked.

"Gravity doesn't go away."

"A law is a law," I told her. "The Perfect Law does not just go away. The Perfect Law does not let an accident slip by anymore than gravity does. The Perfect Law is not a person who can choose. It is a law! It is to be feared reverently (held in high esteem). This is the very reason we are told to be in prayer constantly (1Thes. 5:17). We are to meditate upon God from the time we get up in the morning until the time we go to bed at night, and at all times in between (Deut 6:4-9). God knows all things (Ps 147:5). He has the ability to speak to us and warn us of events as they are about to happen (Amos 3:7). Besides God speaking, there are ministering angels watching over us to deliver us from evil (Ps. 34:7). Those are our messengers and our servants, here to do for us whatever needs done (Hebrews 1:14). They are directed by God (Ps. 103:20). Job could not be touched by Satan because of the protection God had around him (Job 1:7-11). If we lived this way, ignorant mishaps would be prevented."

"So, if he is responsible for the deed, how does he cancel a death?"

"You tell me," I imposed, knowing that if God was not speaking to her, mere logic would prevail.

"You would have to save a life."

"And how would you go about that?" I asked.

"No idea."

"Let's see," I began. "In this country, we could start with the abortion issue. A vote, or a telephone call to your congressman could make a difference. If not, at least your vote would be recorded by the Perfect Law (Prov.6:16-19). In Appalachia and other places here in America, and in most third world countries, there are children dying everyday from malnutrition and starvation. Whenever I hear the number of people dying of starvation I am astonished: Tens of thousands die around the world every day. There are ministries in charge of saving these innocent lives. If you cannot be there to help feed them, perhaps your money can empower someone to go for you. In any event, you are saving lives."

She got it. I report these words so that we can begin to see the questions that might be raised about the Perfect Law, and we can begin to ask our own questions. Only then can God show us the answers and begin to teach us the power and promises of the Perfect Law. We need to contemplate the Perfect Law and take it to the fishing hole in order to uncover its purpose and its work in our own lives. We need to wake up and make our choices known. We have to register our vote with the Perfect Law. No longer can we sit and let our world happen around us. Take control and make goodness, Godliness, and righteousness happen now! Then and only then will goodness come back to us.

Chapter 14
The Anomalies of the Perfect Law of Liberty

UNWARRANTED LAW

Occasionally, something may overcome us that is apparently not the result of a payback for a past deed. I refer to these incidents as "the Job experience," and I draw my conclusions from his story in the Book of Job from the Old Testament. In the opening chapters of the book, God has a meeting with Satan and inquires of him if he has seen what a wonderful, perfect individual His servant Job is. Satan explains to God that Job is only that way because God is protecting him so that Job could not be touched by any evil Satan might present. I suggest that Job is a perfect and upright man with a heart toward God, and Job's own Standard of Measure in righteousness and actions by the Perfect Law kept him from Satan's grasp (Job 1:1,8;2:3). For the sake of showing us Satan's limited power, taking Job to the next level of faith, and proving the Perfect Law, God allows Satan to have full reign over Job and to inflict harm to any degree, excluding death.

As the narrative unfolds, innocent Job loses everything at the hand of Satan. He has done nothing apparent to bring on the events that come against him, yet when you read this book, you will find Job is tested in a way that would cause most of us to surrender. The result of the story is that the Satanic trial is defeated. The test God allows to be inflicted upon Job merely distills Job's knowledge and faith in God. Job has a deeper experience with God, and just as surely, God polishes Job and prepares him for the next level of faith and growth-into-righteousness. When it is all over, everything Job had lost is returned to him and then some.

The story of the crucifixion of Jesus was just as compelling. Jesus might die, but He could never suffer the permanence of death. He was personally innocent and lacked the guilt of having committed any of the Components of Corruption (Sin, iniquity, transgression or trespass) that might allow death to hold Him. Nevertheless, He was accused, beaten beyond measure, and hung on a cross to die. Theologically speaking, Jesus' dying was an actual choice He made to offer Himself in our stead. According to the scriptures, Jesus took our Components of Corruption upon Himself, carried them with Him to judgement, and then gave Himself over to death to be tried. Because Jesus was not guilty of committing by choice any of the Components of Corruption He carried, death could not hold Him (the Perfect Law), His life was returned to Him (the Perfect Law), and the later was greater than the former. What He put out, He got back—only more of it. Jesus gave His mortal life and received life everlasting in return (Acts2:23-32).

Just as in the cases of Job and Jesus, it is not unusual to have our own faith tested or tried by God. (James 1:2-4; 1 Peter 1:7; Ps 7:9, 26:2, 134:23; Prov 17:3; Jer 17:10; 1 Thes 2:4) This is not to be confused with the Act-of-God ideology used by the Kosmos to blame God for our disasters or our sicknesses that come as a return upon our own selfishness. Trials are presented to us or allowed upon us by God for the purpose of proving us. Trials are for distilling our faith and for making us spiritually stronger. Trials have an end, and that end comes with blessing. When a deed comes against us that we know we did not initiate, we must begin to praise God as we ask Him for answers. It may be that the purpose for the unwarranted deed is to introduce a blessing that is yet unseen. Any loss that comes as a result of a trial will be returned according to the Perfect Law by our Standard of Measure. If we know the travail coming against us is undeserved and choose to curse our trial instead of praising the Lord for the event, we may not move to the next level, and we may force ourselves into a rerun. The trial will repeat itself until we are moved to where God has designed us to be.

GENERATIONAL LAW

It would be great if we were innocent of all the evil that comes against us in our lifetimes, but most of the deeds we deal with everyday are the results of our own standards we bring upon ourselves by past actions. On occasion, another kind of unwarranted deed may come upon us that we did not earn. These are deeds caused by something that can be traced to our parents, grandparents, or great-grandparents (second, third, and fourth generation iniquities (Ex. 20:5)). This is an ordeal Bible scholars call a generational curse, and it has come to collect the deed debt of a parent, grandparent, or great-grandparent who passed, having done damage that has not been recompensed.

The most prominent of these generational curses in our society are sex or drug related, especially alcohol. Statistics reveal that growing up with an alcoholic in the house will influence other family members to follow in the same footsteps. According to the Perfect Law, any iniquitous damage done by the alcoholic will result in deeds that must be recompensed or they will be visited upon a descendent. Many alcoholics die as alcoholics, unrepentant and careless. So, family members for generations afterwards may be affected. The same can be said of sexual iniquities such as incest or rape.

Generational curses can arise from any iniquitous deed of a parental ancestor. Murder, abuse, rape, incest, drug abuse, alcohol abuse, or any **deed** that did damage by trespass or transgression must be compensated and forgiven or it is passed down through the generations. Without repentance and recompense, these deeds are guaranteed to return to cause heartache (Num 14:18).

The other side of the generational coin is filled with unwarranted blessings because the Perfect Law is bilaterally just and fair. That means we might also experience generational blessings brought on by our predecessors (Numbers 14:24). Some of us are blessed above what is natural, and are successful in spite of our mistakes. These are the people who can "fall into a bucket of manure and still come out smelling like a rose."

Parents fail to teach their children the constitution of the Perfect Law while they are young. Consequently, many of those who live under the blanket of a generational blessing are unaware of the endowment or have taken it entirely for granted. Have you ever asked the question, "How can that person be so wrong, do such awful things, and yet still be so blessed?" Solomon's story in the Old Testament is a fine example of how the Perfect Law carried a generational blessing forward. Because of his father, King David, Solomon was blessed beyond measure (2Sam. 7:12-17; Ps.132:11-12). However, a full study of Solomon's life will prove that generational blessings do run out (1Kings 11:9-13). They can be undone as a result of current bad deeds erasing the good deeds pushed forward by a predecessor.

When we experience the appearance of evil being blessed, we should assume nothing. We need only to watch and wait. Do not fall victim to the false notion that because we see it happening for someone else, we can do the same. We have no idea upon whose blessing such a person is riding, nor when it will end (Psalm 73).

Though generational curses and blessings may take or give, they can all be undone. No one desires to undo a generational blessing; it is not so with a generational curse. The negative can be undone immediately, and the heir to any curse released through prayer. Before we invoke prayer for release, we should first seek God for knowledge as to why a circumstance has come and how to pray for release. To anyone seeking perfection, God will disclose the purpose and repeal the generational curse. The high purpose for seeking knowledge about a suspect circumstance is to find whether the circumstance is a result of a generational curse or of a trial by God (James 1:5-7). Generational curses usually consist of a series of linear, affiliated, recurring events, and not just a singular occurrence. Alcoholism and child abuse are examples of linear events that should be considered generational curses. I suggest that anyone sustaining a consistent, negative or adverse pattern of events coming against them should seek God for answers and remedies. God is as near as your own prayers. He is not invoked by mediums, seances, palmistry, tea leaves, seers, and the like. God is a mystery only to those who do not know Him and do not speak His language. To those who do know Him, He is closer than a brother (Prov. 18:24). He is inside of us. All we need to do is ask until we get an answer (The mystery of importuning until an answer comes is hidden in Luke 11:2-13). God's answer will come if we ask (Prov. 1; Matt 7:1-11; Prov. 8: 1-21; Matt 13:10-11; Col 2:1-3; Eph. 1:15-19).

It should be mentioned again that generational blessings can be canceled by one's own selfishness. If the choices made create enough negative deeds, they may cancel out any positivity an ancestor might have pushed forward. Generational blessings can flow forward forever if they are realized and maintained by each bearer.

Proverbs 13:22 tells us that a good man leaves an inheritance to his children and to his children's children. This inheritance is not necessarily cash. Most of us have been witness to some young person who, though raised under adverse conditions, went on to success and good fortune because a mother or a father left him a spiritual and moral inheritance.

Generational curses are undeniable. They are, however, arguable as to how they are introduced, how far they will go, and how they can be vanquished. Generational curses are written into the Biblical record both as warnings (Ex. 20:5; Ex.34:7; Num.14:18;Deut. 5:9) and as historical narratives about those who ignored the warnings (2Sam 12:9-10). Those who find themselves arguing the most against generational curses may be those who do not want to face their own guilt and do not want to face the fact that justice will come upon their children by the Perfect Law, should they choose not to repent. To those I say, forgiveness is only a prayer away. Forgiveness is as simple as recognizing the missed mark or the iniquity and asking God to fix it.

Bible scholars might remind us that the Bible clearly states, *The fathers shall not be put to death for the children, neither shall the children be put to death for the fathers: every man shall be put to death for his own sin* (Deut.24:16). This, I suggest, was recorded as a matter of law so that angry individuals could not take revenge on the next of kin. This is not to say our children will not suffer because of our unwillingness to give up our own selfishness to adhere to God's design. This verse in Deuteronomy speaks of death connected to the event of a sin. It does not speak to death in relation to iniquity, or to the death of a child related to the iniquities of the fathers. I might suggest that by the time the father's iniquities are alive in a family, the children have themselves entered into the negativity produced by those iniquities. Now the father's iniquity has become the children's own sin. Again I say, some aspects of these points may be arguable, but it is clear in 1 Kings 15:3 that King Abijam, Nebat's son, *walked in all the sins of his father, which he* (his father) *had done before him: and his heart was not perfect with the lord his God, as the heart of David* . . . There was a reason Abijam followed in his father's footsteps and a reason God bothered to mention it.

A missing of the mark may be hidden in a closet, but an iniquity is not so obscure. Allow me to make this point as I deal with one of the more pervasive problems among our young people today. This is a problem that has come down to us from the generations before us and will continue into the generations that follow if it remains unchecked. I am addressing pornography in this discussion.

Pornography is captivating. Pornography touches every sense in the physical body. Pornography causes lust, and lust is powerful enough to cause a man to overrule the Teacher that is warning him of the danger.

Nathaniel So-and-so has a pornographic magazine hidden in his closet. He visits it often but not so much that he is out of control. Nathaniel, however, has no idea the power of sin to become iniquitous. If the pornography is not put out, Nathaniel's dissatisfaction with the single magazine will lead him to want more. Over time, wanton desire may leave him insensible.

In the primitive state of "it-is-only-one-magazine," it may be difficult for someone to realize that the lust that necessitated that one magazine will grow. For now, it is only closet-hidden-lust. Eventually, it will come out of the closet to reveal itself in Nathaniel's conversations and actions (Matt12:34). If lust is not put out and if the pornography that feeds it is not done away with, lust will eventually rule. The Perfect Law says that if we sow cucumbers, cucumbers will grow. If we sow lust . . .

Lust will not be hidden from the children. The children will see it, and they will *walk in all the sins* of the father. The Perfect Law will see to it (Ps 58:3-5). If we disappoint our Heavenly Father, the Perfect Law will see to it that our children will disappoint us. If our iniquity somehow hurts the child of another, guess what?

As an aside, I should address the fact that we are so messed up in our thinking. Society has chosen an acceptable age for considering someone an adult, and we have accepted it. We have come to believe that we are adults at 18, and by age 21 we should be able to handle the worst that life has to offer. I suggest our adolescent stage is not complete until we reach the age psychology calls "mid-life." That is the age when one begins to review what has gone before to determine what will come next. At this age, many men and women slip back into their childhood one more time to try to keep a hold on what is passing away—their adolescence. Men divorce their wives to look for that younger woman. They trade their car for a motorcycle, and try to drive into the past one last time before becoming an adult. Many a book has been written on the subject. I suggest it is this age that is the true age for the coming of adulthood.

You can trust this as true even though it is my own wisdom: If pornography were not introduced to men and women until after they reached the true age of adulthood, usually around the age of 40, it would not be such a large part of our culture. We could probably say the same of smoking, drinking, drugs, and war. Pornography, sex, drugs, and alcohol are pervasive because they are introduced to adolescent children during the most impressionable years of adolescence. The iniquity that pornography is capable of releasing will be passed down through the generations to follow if it remains unchecked and unchallenged.

FRIENDS AND INFLUENCES

It has often been said we are who our friends are. I suggest this is one of the reasons the Bible instructs us to be careful what we put before our eyes and ears (Ps 101). We might add, "who" we put there, as well. I can remember many times in my youth when I would come in from a hard day of play and my mother would ask me, "You have been hanging around with Martin again, haven't you?" Then she would say, "I can always tell when you are with him because when you come home, you act just like him!"

We are influenced in our daily choices by what we see, what we hear, and the people most associated with it all. Music is people singing a message. Politics are people proliferating a message. Religion is people preaching a message. People use television, radio, newspapers, books, magazines, albums, and the internet to deliver their messages. The Holy Scriptures are God speaking a message.

Jesus told us, *"For where your treasure is, there will your heart be also"* (Matt 6:21). He was telling us that we will be influenced by the objects of our desire. Our computer-like brains were designed to absorb.

We are like little computers waiting to be programed. What we see becomes a part of us. We become a part of who we listen to, run with, and choose to befriend. We take upon ourselves the morals and ideals of what we read, hear, and watch. Outside influences can enter in so subliminally that sometimes we fail to see them coming. We are often not even aware we are being changed by these outside influences.

God warns us in Mark 4:24 to be careful what we listen to. I suggest we also do as King David did and choose to set no wicked thing before our eyes (Ps. 101). There is a reason simple narratives like the story in Genesis 30: 25-43 are given to us. These narratives are designed to show us the power the mind has over the body and how that mind is fooled by what our eyes see or what our ears hear. If there was no need for concern, there would be no Biblical warnings for us to beware what we put before our eyes and ears. The fact is, we are moved and influenced by what we see and what we hear. Marketing works! Commercials work! These are the reasons corporations and conglomerates like Hollywood spend so much money on them. A good marketer knows how to move us from where we are into his other marketplace. Marketers from all walks of life bark their messages. They want us to choose them and their product. I suggest it is easy to be distracted from God and Godly ways by the technical confusion society offers us everyday. We must stay focused and vigilant in our love for God.[1]

A natural man can choose to listen to his own human heart and try to sort the innate truths God has planted in it from the *isms* he has put there himself (Prov. 14:12), or he can scrap it all and choose to let a friend, associate, or even a stranger make his choices for him. Likewise, a S/spirit man can listen to what the Teacher in him is telling him, and go the direction God would have him go (1 John 2:27), or he can scrap it all and choose to let a friend, associate, or even a stranger make his choices for him. When we enter into a friendship or a relationship with another person, organization, or social group, these can influence our choices.

Choice is our tool only as long as we own it and control it. When we relinquish our choice to another, we are signing up for the choices he or she will make for us instead. A deeper study into the words of Leviticus 19:17 will reveal a warning to us that we should rebuke a neighbor, a friend, or brother who is wrong so that we do not become a party in his guilt. This scripture is outlining for us a rule to protect us from the Perfect Law. It is warning us that if we agree with the wrong choices of a friend or neighbor we bind ourselves to his guilt, evil, and ideologies he lives in; the two become one.

This idea of binding ourselves to something and becoming one with it is not limited to personal friendships. When we bind ourselves to a system we become one with that system, and we take to ourselves the baggage and the guilt of that system. An organization, business, political party, city, and government are examples of systems. I am not suggesting that all of these are bad or wrong or that we should not be a party to them. It might become necessary to bind ourselves to something in order to change it; a political party might be a good example. I am suggesting we know what we are binding ourselves to if we are to accept the baggage of these systems. The results could be negative to ourselves and to our children. For instance, when we bind ourselves to a city or region, as Lot bound himself to Sodom (Gen. 13:1-13 esp v.10-11), we should prepare to have an earthquake, whirlwind, or fire from heaven hit it if the neighborhood is foul to God (Genesis 18:16 through 20:26). If we are not paying attention at the time of a nearing calamity, our innocence may become a statistic in the catastrophe. It might be better to live in a cave in the wilderness than in a metropolitan area with people who shake their fist at God and bind together to remove His name and words from their public places and memories (read Psalm 2 in this light).

UNFRUITFUL COVENANTS

Let us consider one last major cause of deed creation in our lives. Some of the deeds that confront us are due to relationships we might enter into that are more than friendships. According to the Bible, when a man and a woman enter into a sexual relationship (married or not), spiritually (in God's reality, where God lives, in God's eyes), that is the consummation of a covenant, and just like a marriage covenant, the two persons who merge are joined together to become one (Gen. 2:4; Matt. 19:4-6; Eph. 5:31). The apostle Paul spoke to just such an event when he was schooling wayward Christians about dropping by the local brothel. *Know ye not, that your bodies are members of Christ? Shall I then take the members of Christ and make them the members of a harlot? God forbid. What! Know ye not that he which is joined to an harlot is one body? For two, saith he, shall be one flesh* (1 Cor 6:15-16). Paul is speaking here of a one-time event of entering into a covenant and binding the Anointing in a Christian to a one-night-stand. In essence, it is a marriage, a covenant between two people.

When we "marry" someone in this way we become one with them, and whatever baggage our mate was carrying when the marriage was consummated is now one with us. All of that person's deeds—good or bad—are to be equally shared by us, even if they were pushed forward from third and fourth generation predecessors we have never met. Can you imagine why someone who has a lot of negative baggage would choose to be so loose with his or her sexuality? Knowledge of the Perfect Law is most likely suppressed, and he or she is not consciously thinking about dividing his or her negative baggage in two and giving half to someone else to carry. However, his or her fallen, self-surviving human nature is aware and is persuaded to make that selfish, "I-must-save-myself" choice. According to the Perfect Law, such a person will most likely find someone with more baggage than him or herself and take on the other's, but I write these pages as a warning not to become the odd one out. The pure and clean individual who chooses to enter into a covenant with a not-so-pure individual will share in his or her nightmare.

"No!" We might scream. "Not Fair! God would not do that!" My friends, God **does not do that!** We do by our own freewill when we choose to enter into that relationship. God designed only the Law that causes the exchange of baggage between two people entering into covenant together. God did not design us to become a partner to unfruitful covenants. That is our choice. Any negative or guilt feelings after such an encounter may be the feeling caused by outside baggage entering into our spirit.

God designed the Perfect Law long before Adam ventured forward from the Garden of Eden. Adam's first son, Cain, was well aware of the existence and the power of the Perfect Law clear back at the beginning of recorded history (Gen. 4:14). God has been tutoring the world in the attributes of the Perfect Law and the Standard of Measure for six thousand years. He has even made it innate in our spirit so that everyone is aware of it. Do not be deceived. Just because we have chosen to live in denial does not mean gravity quit working. No matter what we choose to believe about it or what opinion we might have, gravity works! Likewise, without passion and without prejudice, since the beginning of time, the Perfect Law has been working. It is universal, transcendent, equal, just and fair. It works every time because a law is a law.

The Perfect Law is moseying on, slowly eradicating all of the evil from our world. With the release of this manual, the knowledge of how to invite God into our dominion will cut to the quick and allow the Perfect Law to go to work immediately. The pace of the removal of evil will be greatly increased. All of those people who live by selfish gain without a care about the wake of destruction they leave behind, are about to discover the power of the Perfect Law. As men and women of God join together in obedience and begin to pray as 2 Chronicles 7:14 suggests, the Perfect Law will be released to perform its perfecting power NOW! The Perfect Law was designed to remove evil and nurture Godliness.

I realize this may be difficult for some of us to hear, but a law is a law. No matter how much we want to deny gravity, it will always be there to help us fall down until we learn how to use it to our advantage. We should not deceive ourselves about any of God's laws. God will not be mocked! We will reap what we sow! When God drove the signposts against fornication, adultery, and sexual misbehavior into the ground, they were rules at the edge of a cliff. We can ignore the rules if we choose, but just beyond the—"thou shall not commit adultery or fornication"—is judgement and punishment without prejudice. That cliff is a real and present danger. Be assured, one of the end results of a marriage, permanent or momentary, is that the baggage of the two consummating that marriage is shared. This is a consequence of the spiritual law of binding—**the two shall become one.** The baggage is the deeds of the person to whom we have bound ourselves. In those old days our mothers and fathers talk about, it used to be important to meet the parents of a future mate. It was important to get to know the family and to date the prospective mate long term before entering into a solid contract of marriage. Now we know why!

As an aside, I like to instruct young adults in the knowledge of the Perfect Law concerning their future mates. This is a good lesson for single and married adults as well. Young men—let us take the Perfect Law to the fishing hole in our meditations. Before we ogle any young lady, consider that someday that young lady is going to be a wife to somebody, and perhaps a mother to his children.(I hope to alert young ladies to this lesson as well.) Every person is the prospective mate of some other person, and we must all be sensitive to that fact. Young men, should you choose to look upon a young lady with evil or lustful intentions, the Perfect Law sees it and will deliver the same back to you. Know that some man is looking at your future wife and the mother of your children with the same intentions, only more so. To protect ourselves and those we love or will love, we should avoid any situation that might offer temptation. Lust is powerful, so we must choose not to put ourselves in a position to be subject to it. According to Philippians 2:3, a man or woman of God considers others above self. This is one S/spiritual impetus inside of us that empowers us to make the right choices concerning other human beings. Another impetus should be respect for your future mate! Love them enough to keep them from harms way by avoiding situations that might bring your own standard upon them.

To protect our friends, we should advise them about the consequences of entering into such frustrations. By our objecting to and advising against these "short term marriages," we are protecting someone's future spouse. The Perfect Law sees our actions and will return the same to us. Others will step in to advise against hurting our future mates.

Young adults—know that when you enter into a sexual relationship with some other person's future mate, that someone will enter into a sexual relationship with your future mate. Adult married men—when you have intentions toward another man's wife or lust after a young lady half your age, know that some man or men are looking at your wife or your daughters with like intentions. Adult married women—the Law works for you as well.

Young people—do not wait! Begin now to pray for the physical, emotional, and spiritual health and welfare of your future mates. And share this concept with your peers. As a ruler of the Earth, by our asking, God will place His Angels of protection around our mates. They can be spared much pain. By our own actions we set the standard, and the Perfect Law **will** deliver. The Perfect Law says that if we do not, then it cannot be done to us!

THE SUMMATION OF DEED CREATION

The Job experience is certainly a source of some of the deeds that ambush us. Generational curses and blessings pushed forward from our ancestors, one, two, or three generations before can also present us with some unexpected surprises. The primary source of the deeds that come back to us on a daily basis, however, are most often the results of our own past choices. Becoming aware that those things we have done in the past are the cause of those things that will come against us in the future will cause our conscious mind to better manage our decisions and to make better choices. Becoming aware that deeds of the past relate to deeds of the future will also help in deciphering why the events of our lives do occur and why our world and the world at large is unfolding the way it is. Therein lies the definitive answer to that age old question "Why is this happening?"

When we begin to understand all of the reasons an event can happen (self-inflicted, generational, Job experience), then we can begin to search for answers in our own life. When we invoke God's help by asking for it, He will make clear to us why our events have come upon us. We will find that as we examine our negative past deeds, we will be able to pair those events with negative deeds returned and see God's love in the cancellation.

In our search, we may find deeds and events that have yet to be returned upon us, deeds that need to be vanquished and undone in advance through prayer and compensation. Take advantage of the delay in return and acknowledge God's merciful, loving kindness in permitting the delay. Then seek to disassemble any negative return by repentance and by offering the positive alternative that will negate the deed, praising God all of the while. As each deed is erased, we are one step closer to the "fifty-yard line" of spiritual freedom, that place where no return of negative deeds is due except those we make for ourselves today. The fifty-yard line of a football field is right in the middle. From that position it is as far from one goal post as it is from the other. From that position, by our own choice, we can move to win or we can move to lose.

Truth be known, when we are guilty of trespassing against a neighbor or transgressing the law, we know it. We can hide our sins, transgressions, trespasses, iniquities, and even our deeds. We can hide them from our mother and our brother, but we cannot hide them from God (Is 29:15-16;Jer 23:23-24; Luke 16:15), and we cannot hide them from ourselves (Eccl. 7:21; Ps 4). This may be a difficult truth to accept, but each of us is exactly where we want to be in this life by our own choices. Life is perfectly fair. Some of us may be born into negative places, but we can choose to rise above them. I can assure you by the words in the Bible and by experience with the Almighty, man was designed with the ability to rise above any negative circumstance. For as long as we experience the reality of this world, the pain and suffering of sin is always going to be knocking at our door, wherever that door may be. Rich or not, beautiful or not, intelligent or not, talented or not, we can rise above any circumstance. To say we cannot is to call God a liar (1 Cor 10:1-13). It is to say God cannot help us to overcome our circumstance or God's love is conditional and He does not care for each of us equally. (Phil. 4:11-13).

Some of us are in a negative place because of denial, not wanting to admit the place we reign is the place selfish little i am has chosen to be. Some of us start out in a negative place because our parents or grandparents were poor, prejudiced, cursed, or foolish. But we have always been able to change our own circumstances. Contrary to humanistic beliefs, this is not a "man's world." This is not a "white man's world." This is not a "rich man's world." The world we live in is our world. We own it! We alone control our circumstances. I suggest we never let anyone tell us otherwise. This world is our world, and we have Almighty God standing behind us to ensure that we succeed! We are exactly where we want to be by our own choices. God can give us an idea today that will make us millionaires tomorrow. He can stop the hand of the abuser from ever harming us again, but not if we sit on our choice and do nothing. We need to do something with what we have been given. If you are in such a position, begin now to ask God for help, wisdom, and the knowledge of how to overcome the situation.

We are all responsible for our own fate. That is the design of freewill with its built in Perfect Law and Standard of Measure regulators.

It is the result of **God allowing** man to rule his own life, to have dominion. Free-will is an attribute of man and is man's most important asset. Because this attribute allows us the right to do anything we choose, we must become acutely aware of the cause and effect principal that guides the privilege of free-will and then use it advantageously. The gates of Hell cannot prevail against the man or woman of God who is committed to the purpose and design for which he or she was created. Be Perfect! As your Father in Heaven is Perfect! Choose wisely!

NOTES

1. There are those who claim television, movies, and video games have no effect on the minds of children and young adults. If that were true, commercials would not work and those who use them to their advantage would not spend a dime on them. If the designers of such have any love for their own children, they need to beware how they influence the children of another. Do unto others as you want others to do unto you and expect the return.

Chapter 15
Deed Recompense

Does God dismiss, without recompense, the deeds we have done, or must we answer for each and every one of them? This is the same question posed by the advocate when she asked, "Are a Christian's deeds sometimes overlooked because they are Christians?" Before we talk about deed remission let us review what the Bible has to say about deeds and God's participation in them.

Eccl. 12:13-14 *Let us hear the conclusion of the whole matter: Fear God, and keep his commandments: for this is the whole duty of man. For God shall bring every work* (deed) *into judgment, with every secret thing, whether it be good, or whether it be evil.* Jer. 17:10 *I the LORD search the heart, I try the reins, even to give every man according to his ways, and according to the fruit of his doings* (deeds). Matt 16:27 *For the Son of man shall come in the glory of his Father, with his angels; and then he shall reward every man according to his works* (deeds). Rom 14:10-12 *But why dost thou judge thy brother? or why dost thou set at nought thy brother? for we shall all stand before the judgment-seat of Christ. For it is written, As I live, saith the Lord, every knee shall bow to me, and every tongue shall confess to God. So then every one of us shall give account of himself* (his works or his deeds) *to God.* 1 Cor 3:11-15 *For other foundation can no man lay than that is laid, which is Jesus Christ. Now if any man build upon this foundation* (the Christ foundation) *gold, silver, precious stones, wood, hay, stubble; Every man's work* (deeds) *shall be made manifest: for the day shall declare it, because it shall be revealed by fire; and the fire shall try every man's work* (deeds) *of what sort it is. If any man's work* (deeds) *abide which he hath built thereupon, he shall receive a reward. If any man's work* (deeds) *shall be burned, he shall suffer loss: but he himself shall be saved; yet so as by fire.* Rev 22:12 *And behold, I come quickly; and my reward is with me, to give every man according as his work* (deeds) *shall be.*

If we read only the "law" of the Bible apart from the theme of the Christ, any hope for freedom from the consequences of our deeds will fade. However, a study of the whole of the Bible will reveal that God has made a way for all of our deed debts to be expunged without recompense or remuneration. The emphasis is on the word **can.** When we see our failings and turn from our own selfish ways to God's ways, God can erase anything and everything; however, erasure is according to our choice for repentance.

Repentance can be described as having a consciousness of guilt over sins of the past (missed marks) and with abandon, turning from those old ways to devote oneself to amending the future; realizing our sins (missed marks), recognizing the righteous way and changing the old way of doing things that led us to our missed marks, to do instead something altogether new and different, never to return to the old ways.

According to the Perfect Law, when we turn, God turns. When we forgive, God forgives. When we repent of our un-Godliness, God "repents" of His "judgement" toward us. We get back according to what we put out . . . the Perfect Law. This one Law rules and runs nearly every event that comes upon us.

King David was guilty of murder and should have faced the death penalty. David recognized his transgressions, trespasses, and iniquity, and he realized against Whom these were committed. He immediately repented and turned from his wicked ways. He was delivered from the deed being returned upon him. Though David had killed, he would not be killed. God rescinded David's sin debt and the deed that accompanied it. The deed did not return to him. True repentance was his Standard of Measure and the Perfect Law was disabled. David lived to old age and died in peace.

So, where did the deed go? David still had a deed debt to be paid. When any sin or iniquity or trespass or transgression has its way, a deed is created, and that deed enters our physical reality as a living entity. That deed debt must be recompensed. No deed can be undone. All deeds require compensation. That is the demand of the Perfect Law. It is absolute. There can be no other way.

So, how did God eliminate King David's sin debt while remaining true to Himself and the scriptures? Where did King David's deed debt go? Now we get down to the subject of the depth of God's unconditional love. How far will God's passion for creation go? To what end will God carry His forgiveness of our waywardness? David was spared the consequences of his actions, and did not have to pay for his most heinous crime. The death of Uriah was no longer held against him, spiritually or in the physical world where David caused the deed to become a living entity. However, according to the Perfect Law that cannot sort out David's deed to be overlooked, that "living" deed had to be recompensed.

Enter Jesus, the innocent, the one death could not hold. When Jesus offered Himself to God in our stead, the Bible tells us He took all of our sin debts to Himself. The very nature of sin, along with every unpaid deed, joined with Jesus on the cross. His act was and is an eternal event which annulled all of mankind's past, present, and future debts to sin. Jesus' choice to take our place—to receive our evil deeds upon himself—made Him responsible to God for any punishment that would come of them.

God punished all of the sins of man and destroyed sin itself, but the wrath that destroyed the sin of man fell also upon the S/spirit man who carried those sins and the nature of sin to the "alter of sacrifice." Through the sacrifice made by Jesus, all of the sin debts of every man who chooses to recognize what was done for him on the cross, were absolved. The specifics of how that was accomplished, why that was done, and how we receive that annulment (personally) of all of our own components of corruption are subjects centric to the Bible. It is a love story between God and creation, a love story that will forever remain unequaled.

The annihilation of evil and its corruptive power over mankind, and the annulling of all of man's sin debts were necessary to make man blameless before God. Only then could man once again be enjoined to God as was Adam in the Garden of Eden, S/spirit to s/Spirit. This was the whole purpose for the birth, death, and resurrection of Jesus. It is the theme of the Bible and countless other books. It is the story told day after day, week after week by witnesses who have experienced the forgiveness of God for themselves.

Jesus is not the focus of this treatise. I did not undertake this calling to convert, convict, or proselytize. Be assured, however, and not because I said so, but because Jesus declared it, *"IT IS FINISHED!"* (John 19:30). For any and all who recognize Jesus has taken their sin debt to Himself and who thank Him for doing so, for removing their guilt (caused by an unusual consciousness of sins, iniquities, trespasses and transgressions), He will set them free (Romans 3:23; 6:23;5:8-9;10:8-10, 13). All that is required is a sincere repentance from the heart and a desire to turn from our own selfishness to God's design for us (our purpose in the Earth as it was designed by God Himself) (Isa. 53:10-11; Matt1:21; Romans 3:24-26;4:25; Col. 1:12-14). Then we must invite Him into our dominion by asking Him for help.

Bear in mind, God knows all things, even future things. He knows real repentance because he looks only upon the heart of man, not what the man is telling others or how he is acting (Prov 21:2). When God "sees" repentance, He acts upon it sooner than immediately. We might say forgiveness is granted even before it is asked. (Matt. 6:8)

Oh, how we ignore God. We take the Words of God so lightly. Then we suffer and blame Him for all of our ills as if God made us choose the offensive music we listen to or the indecent videos and movies we watch. God is not causing our problems. We are. As an example, communications on our *public* airwaves used to be policed to protect an innocent public from negative exposure that might promote evil. Now, Not-God secular money moguls cry "first-amendment rights" so they can poison society's morals. They come into our houses through our television sets with their knives and guns and pornography, and we let them in as if they were our friends. By saying nothing, by supporting the negativity they promote, we join them in promoting evil and bind ourselves to their evil deeds. This is an unfruitful covenant and will come back to bite us if we do not repent and remove these indecencies from our homes, our schools, our businesses, and our lives. The Perfect Law is watching every twitch of our eyes and every movement of our hands (Matt 5:29-30 It is easier to cast away your cable, your "R" rated CDs or DVDs, or your tabloids than to harm your own body.). When we choose to stop supporting industries that promote Not-God human secularism, negativity, and evil, they will cease to exist. They cannot continue without our money. If we do nothing, we have made our decision against Godliness and for evil. The Perfect law sees. When we take sides with those who promote evil, purchasing their products or tuning in their messages, we become one with them. We gave them our dominion choice, and now we will reap what they are sowing for us. God will not cause our prosperity if we are asking him for help **while holding** on to our iniquities (James 1:5-7). God cannot take back His words, so He cannot undo the Perfect Law He set into motion.

Negative deeds hang off some of us like blossoms on a flowering tree in springtime. The pain and anguish that come back upon us as a result of our choices to bind ourselves to evil or to others who promote evil can destroy our relationships, cause us to doubt our faith, limit our success, and drain our prosperity. Eventually our poor choices can ruin our life. Is there a way to overcome? Is there a way to rid ourselves of the evils that present themselves to us. Is there a way to turn our life around, removing all of those sins and negative deeds that can cause future heartaches for ourselves or for our children?

Oh, how easy is the return to God. He has made our way of return to righteousness so painless and simple. Man has made it so complicated. We believe ourselves to be so accomplished, so intelligent; surely God must be infinitely more so. Our imaginations make Him unreachable, unknowable, super beyond our finite ability to realize Him. Our imaginations make the way to God much more difficult than God designed. Although there is a gulf between God and man, God has chosen to make Himself available and accessible to us. Though the way to accessibility was difficult to consummate (accomplished by the death, burial, and resurrection of Jesus, and every event from the beginning of time that led up to these events), the door has been opened between God and man, and access to God by man is readily available. We need only to ask Him (Matt. 7:7-12 ends with the mention of the Perfect Law).

The way to know God is so simple it is a stumbling block to those who think God is far and away and difficult to know (1Cor.1:18-25). God has blessed the pathway for those who will see it and choose to put themselves upon that road to perfection (Matt. 11:28-30). God is no respecter of persons (2 Sam. 14:14, 2 Chron. 19:7, Acts 10:34, Romans 2:11). His love for us is unconditional. God never considers our status, be it prom queen or mass murderer (2Chron 19:7; Romans 2:11). There is always a way home. There has always been a way home for everyone because God is love—unconditional love—and that love never fails. All we need to do is repent, turn from our wicked ways, and ask Him to show us His way.

If we are understanding the substance of this message and the importance of the Perfect Law, and if this message is reaching our heart and we are concerned about our soul, there is more good news. It begins with the words, "We are still here!" The fact that we are still here is God's way of saying there is still time to undo all the negative that has been done and to correct those things that need correcting. It makes no difference how far we have fallen. If we are alive, we have not passed the point of no return. There is hope (Eccl. 9:4). Once we are past that point of no return, the point at which there are not enough days left for us to undo all the evil we have accomplished . . . well, bub-bye.

If we need to see that seemingly hopeless lives can be turned around, we can study the accounts of the people of the Bible, like the woman by the well (John 4), the man who waited thirty-eight years for an angel to stir the waters (John 5), and Zacchaeus (Luke 19). Some of these people were so helpless and so overwhelmed with their circumstances they had lost all but hope. Imagine yourself in the footsteps of someone like Legion (Mark 5).

The idea that we still have time and can turn our lives around, and the idea that when time wears out so do we, is straight from the Bible. We can exegete the idea of running out of time from a scripture early on in Genesis, recorded during the covenant cutting session between God and Abram. In Genesis 15:16, God uses the phrase *for the iniquity of the Amorites is not yet full.* Now this is a study that has filled many text books, but the simple idea captured in these few words is that **in-**

iquity is measurable and **it is measured**, suggesting that there comes a time when **the measure is full** and **the end of measuring has come**. The fate of the world by the flood in Noah's day, the fate of Sodom, the fate of the nations of Israel and Judah are historic examples of iniquity being filled and time running out. These were destroyed because of choices made to ignore God's leading; men chose Not-God over God. Their judgements were delivered according to the Perfect Law, however, the punishments were carried out by floods, hailstorms, and in the cases of Israel and Judah, by other nations that were equally evil but whose iniquities had not yet been filled up. When these destroyer nations' iniquities were filled up, these nations were also destroyed, and they were destroyed by the same methods with which they destroyed others. All was accomplished by the Perfect Law.

If we convert this idea of not-too-late to an understandable scenario, we might liken it to the point of no return in an airplane flight over the ocean. There comes a point in the flight when the plane becomes committed because too many miles have been traveled and the remaining fuel is not enough for the return trip home. Likewise, in our "flight" from our own birth to our own death, if there are not enough days remaining in our lives for us to undo all the negative we have created, our iniquity is full and it is time for judgement. Bub-bye. But know this, and be assured of it: If you are still among the living, our loving, forgiving God is waiting and wanting you to make the turn around, and there is still time. Today is the day of salvation (2 Cor 6:1-2). The scripture says God has granted you grace up until now. Do not ignore His offering of forgiveness or hesitate another moment to acknowledge Him. Repent and ask God to perfect your life. Now!

Where do we go for lessons on repentance? We go to the same book; we go to the Bible. As an example, study this scripture and meditate upon it. Romans 8:13 *For if ye live after the flesh, ye shall die: but, if ye through the Spirit do mortify* the **deeds** of the body (or flesh), *ye shall live.*[1]

This verse in Romans speaks directly to the use of the Spirit to mortify or do away with deeds of the flesh. Deeds of the flesh are deeds done according to the fallen nature of man, a nature unlike the nature of God. Deeds of the flesh are humanistic, selfish, and lacking in Godliness. Such deeds can be heinous or they can be the simple things we do everyday such as eating our food without thanking God for it (1 Thes. 5:16-19), being disrespectful to our elders (Exodus 20:12; Eph. 6:1-3), mocking God by insulting our presidents or our governments that are chosen and put in place by God to oversee us (Dan 2:21, Rom. 13:1-7), hoarding our wealth (2 Cor 9:6-15) or hoarding our love (and I am not talking about withholding love from only those who love us) (Luke 6:27-36).

There are two ways to mortify the deeds of the flesh. One of them is repentance. We can repent and ask God to erase those things we cannot remove ourselves—murder, for instance. We may not be able to make the dead live again, but God is able remove the deed we created if we choose to repent. Just as He did with King David, He can dispose of our deed debt by displacing it into the Lord Jesus Christ.

The second way is deed cancellation. Make restitution for any deeds created, and do that by over doing it. If we stole ten dollars, return twenty. If we killed one, save ten. We must be particularly sensitive to those who might have been hurt by our past actions. The damage done to them must be undone through repentance, forgiveness, and compensation.

There is a deeper design to deed cancellation. The knowledge of this design is a treasure buried within Romans 8:13. It is a hidden mystery not everyone may comprehend readily.

Romans 8:13 specifically states that the deeds of the flesh will be mortified by the Spirit. Deeds mortified by the Spirit implies we focus upon God, concentrate on the things of today, and let God deal with the mortification of deeds (Matt 6:34). I suggest this type of deed compensation is meant to cover over those deeds we cannot possibly undo ourselves because the people we harmed are gone or we have lost track of them over the years, or the things we did are impossible to compensate. The Apostle Paul was sent to us as an example of this type of deed elimination. As a result of his own actions, it became Paul's privilege to be God's example to us.

The Apostle Paul was permitted to be a steward over most all of God's mysteries and a benefactor of God's deliverance from his own deed debts that were returned upon him with interest. God did not deliver Paul **from** the return of his deeds as He did David, but God delivered Paul **through** these returned deeds. God allowed Paul's deeds to return upon him to keep him from boasting of himself or as Paul put it—*lest I should be exalted above measure* because of *the abundance of the revelations* he had received (2Cor 12:7). After all, Paul was the gate-keeper of the New Testament and that was the reason so much of it was authored through him. His deeds done in the flesh were mortified by the Spirit as he performed the will of God for his own life. All this is apparent through a study of Paul's life in the book of the Acts of the Apostles and from his epistles in the New Testament.

Paul's story is a wrenching one. As Christianity was spreading throughout the Middle-East, certain Jews in Paul's time felt their religion was being threatened and were driven to defend their Jewish faith against what they saw as heresy—the Christian religion. Paul was a leader among this group, and he believed he was doing God's will by hurting or killing innocent Christians in order to silence them. Paul moved from town to town in the name of God, by orders of His "church," seeking to find and punish those who did not believe his way. He would have them beaten, thrown into prison, or, as in the case of Stephen, stoned to death (Acts 7).

After Paul's conversion to Christianity, he spent his life traveling from town to town as an evangelist, teaching the exact same message for which he had others brutalized. Paul was continually persecuted. His enemies, like the band of Jews he used to belong to, would hunt him down, throw him into prison, try him before the courts, have him beaten or scourged, and by his own affirmation, even stoned (and we can suppose, left for dead). Paul's testimony in 2 Corinthians 11, beginning with verse 23, tells us he was beaten so many times he lost count. He had suffered the punishment of stoning; five times he was scourged with 39 lashes; three times beaten with rods; and the list goes on. Paul was God's right hand man of the New Testament. He is considered by scholars to be the Moses of the New Testament. Surely God would overlook his missed marks, or at least displace them into Jesus.

In spite of all he suffered, Paul was blessed beyond measure. He said so in 2 Corinthians 7. He said he had been given so many revelations from God that he should be exalted above measure; however, to keep him from becoming haughty and high-minded, God allowed a thorn in Paul's flesh (2 Cor. 12:1-10). It seems that by the power of the Perfect Law, a messenger of Satan was allowed to follow Paul everywhere he went to make sure he was buffeted, meaning beat with a fist. Paul asked God to remove his deed debt and to chase away the evil messenger. God said (paraphrasing), "No! My grace is sufficient. I will take care of you to deliver you **through** these incidents." And God did. Paul ran his race, worked his ministry, took his punishment, and even when stoned and left for dead, got up and walked on. I suggest what Paul received was a little more than what he himself had put out over the years.

This is an example of a man who did the worst of things a man can do to his fellow man. He asked God for total debt removal for all of the foolish deeds he had committed, and God answered him with a "no." God explained to Paul that His grace was sufficient enough to see Paul through any return of deed (2Cor 12:9). That answer was not the answer Paul expected; however, over time, it proved to be the better way. Surely every time a deed returned upon Paul and he was delivered from or through it, his faith must have doubled. Over the course of His tenure, Paul's faith became unshakeable. By the commitment of Grace, God promised Paul that he would be delivered through all of the hardships and that he would finish his race as it was designed. Paul did just that (1Tim 4:6-7).

The message of Paul's thorn in the flesh should also be a lesson to us. If Paul, a pillar of the first century church and the man responsible for much of our New Testament was not spared from the Perfect Law, neither will we be. Do not be deceived. What we sow, we will reap.

NOTES

1. Let me suggest a form of meditation for those of you who seek to find the depth of a scripture. Take a verse like the one just mentioned, and highlight each word, one at a time, putting an emphasis on a different word each time you say the whole scripture. Begin with the first word, and say the entire verse out loud. Now, do it again, this time putting the emphasis on the second word. Read it through completely, then move to the third word, and so on.. Example: ***For*** *if ye live after the flesh, ye shall die: but, if ye through the Spirit do mortify the deeds of the body, ye shall live. For **if** ye live after the flesh, ye shall die: but, if ye through the Spirit do mortify the deeds of the body, ye shall live. For if ye live after the flesh, ye shall die: but, if ye **through** the Spirit do mortify the deeds of the body, ye shall live.* Each time you say the verse, think about what it means and how the verse has changed by emphasizing a different word. By the time you are finished doing this with every word in the verse, you should know the meaning of the verse.

Conclusion

Now you have it. With the exception of the two rules set in place to guide the Perfect Law toward goodness, you know the constitution of the Perfect Law. I did not intend to spend any time explaining the two rules that guide it because they are totally self-explanatory once you understand the Perfect Law and how it works. These are the two rules that guide it: 1 *Thou shalt love the Lord thy God with all thy heart, with all thy soul, and with all thy mind,* 2 *Thou shalt love thy neighbor as thyself* (Matt. 22:36-40). Our *neighbor* can be our closest friend, a complete stranger, or our worst enemy. If I were to interpolate these two rules, I would say they mean this: Know God with everything in you (which includes learning the language of Bible), and treat others as you would want to be treated yourself. These rules are just rules, and we can choose to ignore them, but my calling was to inform us all that life's events in this reality are subject to one law and two rules. Do with them as you please.

After we have understood the Perfect Law and the two rules that guide it toward the positive, we may begin to experience the countless promises the Bible says are ours according to choice, according to free-will, and by our own Standard of Measure. Many of these promises recorded in the Bible come with qualifiers that explain in detail what to expect. These promises are most often written as rules to inform us that if we do such-and-such, then this other thing will happen. The promises given to us in the Bible comprises everything we will ever need to succeed in God's kingdom here on Earth. God's Holy Spirit, the Teacher within, will advise us of anything we may need beyond these promises. The promises in the scriptures will come naturally to us as we succeed with the Perfect Law and the two rules that guide it. What seemed to be signs and wonders flowing from the Disciples of Jesus as they began their ministries in the first century A.D., were in fact, promises (Acts 2:43; 4:30; 5:12). Such promises of God did not end with the deaths of those original Disciples.

There is much more to be said on this subject. This treatise was designed to open the dialogue and begin studies into the Perfect Law from every genre. No matter what comes of it, be assured of this one thing: Whenever the question *"why did this happen?"* is asked, the Perfect Law is somewhere in the answer. The Perfect Law is the definitive answer. It is the answer to how peace can be found on the earth and how love grows; how evil can be vanquished and how the playing field can be leveled. This Law is written countless times into the pages of the Holy Bible and into the scriptures of every other world religion. It has been placed by God into the spirit of every man, woman, and child ever born. We are without excuse.

What we choose to do with what we now know is entirely up to us. We have discussed how it matters little what we believe about a law or what our opinion of it might be. A law is a law. We have also discussed Adam's second decision at the fall of man away from God's reality. His first choice was to disobey God. His second was to remain in that position, away from God and Godliness (Jer. 2:13-14).

Now we, like Adam, are standing outside the garden of Godliness. The Kingdom of God on Earth awaits our decision. God has been calling to all of us to return to Him for thousands of years. The choice of what to do with our new knowledge will lead us home or take us further from it. That choice is ours. That choice has always been ours. By not choosing, we are choosing. So, choose wisely, and live (Deut. 30:19-1-20).

And if ye call on the Father, who without respect of persons judgeth according to every man's work, pass the time of your sojourning here in fear: (1 Peter 1:17)

So speak ye, and so do, as they that shall be judged by the law of liberty. For he shall have judgment without mercy that hath shewed no mercy; and mercy rejoiceth against judgment. (James 2:12-13)

It is appointed unto men once to die, but after this the judgement: (Heb. 9:27)

Are you ready for your appointment?

(The Beginning)

Appendix
Where Do We Go From Here?

In keeping with my original intent not to convict, convert, or proselytize through this book, those who desire to know where we go from here can consummate this message to themselves by studying the Appendix. The Appendix sanctions the spiritual nature of the Perfect Law of Liberty and advances the "how to" methods to bring about change. The Appendix may be accessed through our website at

www.libertytpl.com/appendix.htm.

Acknowledgments

The Holy Bible—New York: American Bible Society—published 1844 was used to report the majority of the scriptures used in this text. The Holy Bible—published in Philadelphia by C. Alexander & Co. Athenian Buildings, Franklin Place 1839, was used for the remainder.

References to the great American Novel *Gone with the Wind* By Margaret Mitchell ©1936 by Macmillan Company, renewed 1964 by Stephens Mitchell and Trust Company of Georgia

Webster's Third New International Dictionary ©1966 by G. & C. Merriam Co. and *The Compact Edition of the Oxford English Dictionary* ©1971 by Oxford University Press, were used exclusively throughout this work to assure all words were used correctly and for many of the quoted definitions.

Any references or similarities to the works or publications of Bishop Malcolm Smith and Zoe Community of the Holy Spirit are a result of Michael Angelo's adherence to the teachings of Bishop Malcolm Smith. These similarities and references have been acknowledged by Bishop Malcolm Smith and Zoe C.H.S. This is not to suggest or imply any association or affiliation by Bishop Malcolm Smith or Zoe C.H.S. to the teachings in this book or to any other publications by Michael Angelo. Zoe C.H.S , P.O. Box 1599, Bandera, TX 78003. For further references or for extended educational material, the entire catalog of Bishop Malcolm Smith is highly recommended and may be viewed on their website. www.malcolmsmith.org.

Some material has been taken from *Things your Mama Never Taught You About Discipline,* by Michael Angelo ©2000, to be released 2007 by Zugos Publishing Company, P.O. Box 1738 Westerville, Ohio 43086-1738.

About the Author

Great deeds are most often the accomplishments of little people. Who was Alexander before he became "The Great" or Michelangelo before he became a ninja turtle? History is full of characters who recognized the call and filled the need without a desire for the spotlight. God uses such people because they are faithful.

Michael Angelo is one such shadow man; a home-grown American whose grandparents migrated from Romania and Italy in the 1908 and 1909 respectively. He comes from a long line of entrepreneurs, war heroes, and faith-filled people. He was raised as an Evangelical United Brethren, enlightened as a free-will Baptist, and ordained non-denominationally. Michael lends his message to every faith and knows no religious boundaries.

Michael is a renaissance man of sorts; he is a teacher, musician, painter, sculptor, designer, and writer. He is a husband, father, and grandfather. He is very public and very private and knows well how to separate the two. Michael has learned that celebrity and solitude oppose one another and solitude is that place where God can be heard. He is most often there.

Michael may be accessed through his website www.Libertytpl.com

A list of coming books by Michael Angelo may also be found at www.Libertytpl.com

QUICK ORDER FORM

TELEPHONE ORDERS:
Call Toll Free 1-800-975-6403
Have your credit card ready

WEB ORDERS:
www.zugospublishing.com

FAX ORDERS:
Fax the completed order-form
to 1-800-975-6403

POSTAL ORDERS:
Fill out and mail this order-form
with the credit card information
or a check to our Publisher:

Zugos Publishing
Order Department
P.O. Box 1738
Westerville, Ohio 43086-1738

Please send _____ copies of *Liberty—the Perfect Law* to:

Name_____

Address_____

City_____State____Zip_____

Telephone_____ E-Mail _____

☐ Please send me information on future books by Michael Angelo.

PAYMENT

☐ Check enclosed   ☐ Credit Card

☐ Master Card   ☐ Visa   ☐ Discover   ☐ Amex

Card Number_____ Expiration_____

Credit Card issued to_____

Number of copies _____ × $14.95 = Subtotal (1)_____

In Ohio, add 7% sales tax. (Subtotal X .07)   (2)_____
(*Ohio Non-Profit Organizations please supply tax exempt information.*)

Add $2.65 shipping and packaging fee for the first book and $1.85 for each additional copy. (Orders of over 10 copies will be shipped postage paid to a single address.) Total shipping costs (3) _____

Total Amount Due (Add lines 1, 2 & 3 together) _____

For Rapid Shipping, International Shipping, or any questions you might have, please call our Order Department at **1-800-975-6403.**